D0354632

Tropical Fish

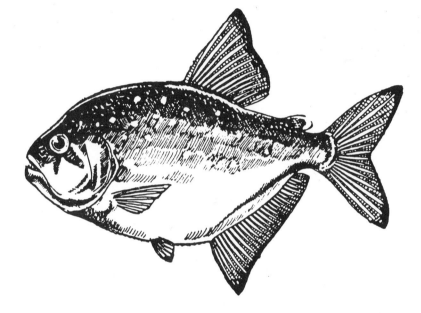

Edited by the staff of *Tropical Fish Hobbyist*® Magazine.

A major portion of the text of this book has appeared previously in the *Advanced Aquarist Guide.* The new edition has been re-edited, updated and illustrated with new color photographs.

© 1984 by T.F.H. Publications, Inc. Ltd. Copyright is claimed for the new material and for the edited version.

Contents

Front cover: Angelfish; photo by A. Roth.
Back cover: *Corydoras* catfishes; photos by Burkhard Kahl.

Captions for posters:
A: A gorgeous blue discus, *Symphysodon aequifasciata*, with its fry. Discus fry feed on mucus secreted by the parents' skin. Photo by Hans-Georg Petersmann.
B: A male tuxedo variatus platy, *Xiphophorus variatus*. Photo by Hans-Joachim Richter.
C: Few fishes can surpass the beauty of a good marigold variatus platy, *Xiphophorus variatus*. Photo by Hans-Joachim Richter.

Aquarium setups of today fit well in any part of the contemporary home. Aquarium tank and equipment design have undergone great changes through the years. One can keep a tank of easy to care fishes at the start that require minimal care and attention.

Introduction

For whatever reason, you have decided to make tropical fishes your hobby. They are restful, interesting, inexpensive and great for kids, but an adult must be the one who supervises what goes on. This book deals only with the fishes that are to be kept in the aquarium. It does not deal with the reasons why one aquarium is better for you than another. This is something you have to work out with your local petshop dealer. Let him show you the sizes and shapes of aquariums that he can offer you; consider the prices of these tanks and the accessories such as a hood with a built in light, filters, pumps, etc. Not everything is necessary. A large tank with a few fish and some beautiful live plants does very well without pumps and filters, but you really have to know what you are doing. If you are a beginner, start with the largest tank you can afford and buy the best filter, pump and heater that is practical. You won't regret it.

If a pump fails, it might result in your losing your whole collection. Follow your dealer's advice. Then, too, ask him this: "If my pump or filter breaks down, will you loan me one until the manufacturer has replaced or repaired the damaged one?" Most dealers will loan or rent one. They usually ask you to pay for it and then they give you a refund when your damaged unit is returned.

The selection of fishes which follows is not by any means an exhaustive list. It is not even a list of the most valuable or the most beautiful fishes. It is just a list of "typical" fishes. This book is merely an introduction to tropical fishes. If you want to really find out what aquarium fishes are available, ask your petshop to show you a copy of *Exotic Tropical Fishes* by Dr. Herbert R. Axelrod and his associates. The expanded edition has color photographs of almost 1,000 aquarium fishes with everything you need to know about them.

Good luck in your new hobby—you are really going to enjoy it.

Your local petshop dealer will always be willing to help and offer suggestions for starting one in the fish hobby.

Classification and Nomenclature

The aim of any classification is to arrange a collection of diverse things into groups and subgroups of similar or related individuals. Thus the individuals in a given group resemble one another more closely than they resemble members of other groups. Such a system not only brings order out of chaos but is also an indispensable aid to clear thinking. The details and intricacies of classification are truly for the taxonomist but what the aquarist needs to know is quite easy to understand.

All the fishes described in this book and virtually all the fishes that aquarists keep belong to the great group of bony fishes called Teleostei. The Teleostei are subdivided into various orders. The orders are subdivided into families, the families into genera, and the genera into species. Our interest as aquarists lies mainly with the last subdivisions, namely, families, genera, and species.

The scientific name of a fish is in fact composed on this basis: the first word in the name of the fish tells us the genus to which it belongs, the second indicates the species. Thus the popular Tiger or Sumatra Barb has the scientific name *Capoeta tetrazona*. There are many other Barbs, such as *Puntius nigrofasciatus* (Black Ruby). Each of these may have more than one common name, depending on local preferences, but only one scientific name which will be accepted world wide and in all languages. Thus each fish has a definite name by which all of us throughout the

You may find that different dealers may give the same fish various common names. It will be best to know the scientific name always, to avoid confusion.

world know it. This is the great virtue of scientific nomenclature in contrast to the popular names we give our fishes. These frequently apply to more than one species. Thus the term Pencil Fish has been employed to describe a number of different fishes belonging to the genus *Nannostomus,* and the terms Glass Fish, Glass Tetra, and X-Ray Fish have been applied in a confusing fashion to many widely different species, apparently the only requirement being that the fish should be translucent or semitranslucent.

Nevertheless there is no harm in using such names among a circle of friends, for each knows what is meant and any ambiguity can be quickly cleared up by asking questions. It would be inadvisable to use such names alone when writing about fishes or lecturing to strange audiences. In this book I have tried as far as possible to give the scientific as well as the most widely known popular names of fishes.

We have now examined the main points regarding classification and nomenclature (both scientific and popular). There are, however, a few points which I omitted in the interest of continuity so let us deal with them now.

Sometimes in a given species we find many color varieties as well as different degrees of fin development. Thus we have many color varieties of Platies, all of which bear the scientific name *Xiphophorus maculatus*.

Sometimes it may happen that we know the genus to which the fish belongs but we do not know the species. For instance, there are believed to be three species of Angelfish—*Pterophyllum altum, P. dumerilii, P. scalare*. If, like most of us, you do not know which particular species of Angel you have, then you could refer to it as *Pterophyllum* sp.

You will have noticed that the first letter of the name of the genus is a capital and of the species a small letter, and also that when the genus is repeatedly mentioned it can be abbreviated as shown above.

So far, the virtues of scientific classification and nomenclature have been stressed; it is only fair to point out that they can be the source of much annoyance and headache to both aquarists and scientists alike.

As ichthyological research continues, fishes have to be reclassified, and old favorites appear under new and unfamiliar names. This is because the nature and relationships have been discovered; we can do nothing about it but learn the new name.

The fishes in this book are arranged in families and the families are arranged in taxonomic order. Thus we begin with the early-evolved Pantodontidae and end with the highly evolved Cichlidae and Anabantidae.

Petshop owners carry both the easy-to-keep fishes for beginners as well as some more demanding species for their advanced customers. Do not hesitate to request that your dealer order a particular fish you wish to have.

The Fishes

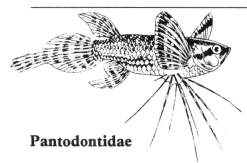

Pantodontidae

There is only one species in this family.

Pantodon buchholzi Peters 1876
Popular name Butterfly Fish, Fresh Water Flying Fish.
Origin West Africa.
Size 4 inches.
Appearance Boat-shaped body with upward-facing mouth. Large winglike pectorals. Greenish gray to brown body with many dark spots and streaks.
Behavior Reasonably peaceful. Can be kept with fishes its own size.
Feeding Will not feed off the bottom. Live insects and small fishes are readily accepted. Can be trained to take worms and other meaty foods from the end of a stick.
Water conditions Prefers moderately soft water at a temperature of 80 °F. Butterfly Fish are best kept in a well-covered aquarium half filled with water, planted with a few thickets of plants that send some shoots above the water surface.
Sexing Posterior end of anal fin shows a notch in the male; same zone straight in the female. When ripe, females show the usual fuller appearance.

Breeding Difficult to breed. At mating the fish wrap themselves around each other and release eggs which float to the surface. Young hatch after three days and need minute insects for their diet.

Mormyridae

These fishes occur commonly in many pools in Central and South Africa. The ratio of brain weight to body weight compares favorably with that in man. They have a remarkable ability for learning and an inquisitive, playful nature. Some of them have weak electric organs. It is important to ascertain that the fish is feeding properly before purchase. Often starved, wasted specimens have been offered. These usually refuse to eat and perish.

Gnathonemus petersi Gunther 1862
Popular name Elephant Nosed Fish.
Origin Congo and Cameroons.
Size Up to 9 inches. In aquaria 4 inches.
Appearance Elongated, laterally compressed body with dorsal and anal fins set well back on the body. Mental (chin) projection surmounted by a small mouth. Over-all coloration dark brown to black with two white bands on posterior part of the body.
Behavior A shy, peaceful fish. Can be kept in a community tank with even small fishes. Other fishes seem to leave it alone. Feeds at dusk, hides most of the day.

 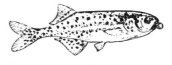

Feeding *Tubifex* and freshly dead *Daphnia* are favorite foods. Will seek all sorts of foods, including dried foods, at the bottom.

Water conditions Fairly soft neutral water at 80°F. Well-planted tank with shady spots and hiding places. Does not like strong light.

Sexing, Breeding Little is known about this. Not bred in captivity.

Marcusenius schilthuisiae
(Boulenger 1899)
Popular name Elephant Trunk Fish.
Origin Middle Congo.
Size 4 inches.
Appearance Similar in appearance to *G. petersi* except that it has a much lighter silvery-brown body with one dark band and a blunt tubercle instead of the elongated chin process. Scales rather prominent.
Behavior, Feeding, Water conditions, Sexing, Breeding Similar to *G. petersi*.

Characidae

Many Characins are distinguished by the possession of a small adipose fin. Also, Characins usually have teeth in the jaws. Like Carps and Catfishes, they belong to the order Ostariophysi: hence they have Weberian ossicles linking the swim bladder with the inner ear. Most of them come from Central and South America, a few from Central Africa. Some of these fishes are carnivores, others are omnivorous, and some predominantly herbivorous. The last will nibble or totally destroy aquarium plants. Most of the aquarium Characins are small species which inflict little damage with their teeth, beyond occasionally nipping the fins of such slower-moving fishes as Angels or Fighters. However, they are closely related to the Piranhas which, with their powerful teeth, can strip the flesh off even large terrestrial animals in a very short time.

The majority of Characins prefer soft peaty water and breed best under such conditions. They lay adhesive or semiadhesive eggs, which they are likely to devour, given the chance.

Some aquarium Characins are easy to breed, most require some skill and knowledge on the part of the aquarist, while a few demand expert treatment. When you have bred these you have really reached the pinnacle of achievement in the aquarist fraternity. It is advisable to separate and condition the fish prior to spawning.

Choosing and Conditioning the Fish

Much of the success in breeding Characins depends on the treatment the fish have received months before actual spawning. In order to breed a given species it is best to obtain half a dozen or more youngsters from a reliable source and then rear them to maturity. When the females begin to fill up with

eggs the sexes are separated for a week or two and given the best in the way of aquarium management and feeding. This process is called conditioning.

The Planted Tank Method

This is perhaps the oldest method of breeding Characins. A small or medium-sized tank of about five or ten gallons is furnished with fine-leaved plants, coarse gravel (1/8″ diameter) or pebbles (1/2″ diameter) and water suitable for breeding the species concerned. Care is taken to see that no snails, planarians, or other egg- or fry-destroying creatures are introduced.

When all is ready the conditioned pair are transferred to the breeding tank. This is usually done late in the evening. By next morning, if all goes well, the fish will have settled and commence spawning. In most species fertilization of the eggs occurs in the water. These then adhere to plants; a few fall to the bottom. The end of the spawning session is heralded by the pair losing interest in each other and starting to browse around in the plant thickets or on the aquarium floor, seeking eggs to devour. At this stage the parents are removed.

The eggs hatch in a few days and the fry can be seen hanging on the plants and the glass wall of the tank. A few days later they become free-swimming. Characin fry are very small and need infusoria as first food.

Method of Breeding Characins on Artificial Spawning Media

Briefly, the main advantage of using artificial spawning media such as willow root and nylon mops over fine-leaved green plants is that with this system one can have a clean, easily reproducible setup free from snails and planarians for breeding fishes.

In this technique for breeding Characins a 5- or 10-gallon tank is first thoroughly cleaned out. Soap, detergents, or chemicals may be used if thoroughly rinsed out as routine; simply scrubbing and rinsing is usually quite adequate. However, there are times when something stronger may be necessary. In such instances I like to use ammonia (specific gravity 0.8), rather than any other chemical. About 50 to 100 ml. of this are added to the tank full of water and allowed to stand a few hours. The ammonia-containing water is now removed and the tank filled and emptied with fresh water five times. This rinses out the ammonia and leaves the tank clean and free from pests and their eggs, all of which are killed by this process.

In the bottom of the tank is now placed an inch layer of boiled pebbles. (Some aquarists like to use glass marbles instead of pebbles, but I do not recommend them as many fish are frightened and refuse to spawn or burrow under them. I have found fish trapped and dead next morning when

using glass marbles in breeding tanks.)

The tank is now filled with tap water, tap water plus distilled water (or rainwater), or peat water as needed for the species. A handful of cleaned and boiled willow root or some nylon mops are introduced. The tank is now ready to receive the conditioned fishes. The procedure from here on is the same as described earlier in breeding Characins in planted tanks.

The Acriflavine Adsorption Method for Breeding Characins

Acriflavine and various other dyes are commonly employed when breeding Cichlids to prevent eggs from becoming covered with fungus. There is another distinct and different way in which this dye can be employed to assist in breeding the problem fishes. The method I am about to describe was first evolved by Jacobs. Later, unaware of this work, I also evolved a similar method . I have used this method extensively to produce large numbers of Glowlights while Jacobs has used it for both Glowlights and Neon Tetras.

For this method a tank is cleaned and filled with suitable water (not treated with peat). Now enough of a solution of acriflavine is added to produce a final concentration of about 1 milligram/gallon in the tank. (The amount is not very critical.) Let this stand for a day or two and then add boiled willow root. The dye will be absorbed by the root and the water will become crystal clear in a few hours. The breeding pair is now introduced. After spawning is completed the pair is removed and the tank covered so as to exclude most of the light. It is thought that strong light will ruin the eggs of some of the more difficult-to-breed Characins. The fry hatch out after a few days and are fed in the usual way. It is interesting to note that with this method both Jacobs and I have been able to breed Glowlights not only in soft acid waters but also in alkaline waters of moderate hardness.

If willow root is not available for adsorption and spawning, a charcoal filter could be used to remove the dye from the water. It is important to remove the dye prior to spawning. If fishes are allowed to spawn in water containing acriflavine the eggs will be infertile, for acriflavine will kill the sperms before they can fertilize the eggs.

Peat Water for Breeding Characins

German aquarists were the first to report that certain difficult-to-breed Characins (problem fishes), such as the Neon Tetra, could be bred successfully in water that had been allowed to stand in contact with peat, oak bark, or oak leaves.

Peat water is prepared by adding

handfuls of scalded peat to a quantity of rainwater. In time the peat sinks and the water becomes amber colored; pH and hardness readings are taken and more peat added if necessary. Over a period of some months pH and hardness value decline.

According to McInnery the final water must have a hardness not exceeding 10 ppm and should ideally be as low as 2 ppm for successful breeding of neons. The pH can be anywhere between 5 and 6.8.

A small, clean tank (preferably but not necessarily all glass) is filled to a depth of 4" or so with this water. No gravel or pebbles are used. Nylon mops serve as spawn receptors. A conditioned pair of Neons is introduced. These should spawn within 24 hours.

Peat water not quite as soft as that used for Neons has been employed for breeding not only difficult-to-breed Characins but also a variety of fishes belonging to other families.

Although many aquarists are convinced of the benefits of peat water or soft acid water in breeding a variety of fishes, there are those who point out that virtually every fish, including Neons, on more than one occasion has also been bred in moderately hard alkaline water. Further, the fact that peat water is soft does not permit us to conclude that this is the factor responsible for success, even though it may serve as a good index for judging the suitability of the water for breeding fishes.

Serrasalmus rhombeus
(Linnaeus 1766)

Popular name White Piranha, or Spotted Piranha.

Origin South America, Amazon Basin.

Size Up to 10 inches. Aquarium specimens 6 inches.

Appearance A deep-bodied, strongly compressed, olive-green to silvery fish, with many strong teeth set in a large mouth with protruding lower jaw giving a bulldoglike appearance.

Behavior Piranhas are aggressive to any fishes, smaller or larger than themselves. Even during transport they will attack other fishes. Best kept as single specimens. Care required when netting. One's hand should not be placed in the tank. This fish, like other Piranhas, must be kept out of reach of children. A good showpiece because of its savage reputation.

Feeding Carnivorous. Other fishes, pieces of lean meat.

Water conditions Not critical.

Sexing, Breeding Not bred in captivity. When a pair are brought together one will probably eat the other!

Serrasalmus nattereri (Kner 1859)

Popular name Red-breasted Piranha, or Natterer's Piranha.

Origin Amazon and Orinoco systems.

Size Up to 12 inches. In aquarium 4 inches-6 inches.

Appearance Perhaps the handsomest and most macabre Piranha. Deeply compressed body, blue-gray with red underside. Numerous metallic spots.

Behavior, Feeding, Water conditions, Sexing, Breeding Same as for *Serrasalmus rhombeus.*

Metynnis lippincottianus
(Cuvier 1870)
Popular name Silver Dollar.
Origin Amazon Basin.
Size 5 inches.
Appearance One of the most popular *Metynnis* species available. Strongly compressed oval body with length slightly greater than depth.
Behavior A shy, peaceful, schooling fish best kept in the company of its own kind in a large tank. A predominantly herbivorous fish which destroys aquarium plants rapidly. A single specimen will mow down a tank full of *Vallisneria* within a few days.
Feeding Vegetable food such as lettuce, spinach, and sprouts should be provided. Must also be given some standard meaty fresh foods.
Water conditions Slightly acid, moderately soft water.
Sexing, Breeding Bred on only a few occasions. The anterior portion of the anal fin is markedly convex in the male but angular in the female. At spawning time the caudal and anal fins show a bright red border surrounded in the case of the caudal by a black margin. Approximately 200 eggs are laid. These hatch in a few days. Fry become free-swimming four to five days later and are easily reared on the usual foods plus vegetable material.

Metynnis hypsauchen (Muller and Troschel 1844)
Popular name Schreitmueller's Metynnis.
Origin Amazon Basin.
Size 6 inches.
Appearance Strongly compressed oval body, with length slightly greater than depth.
Behavior, Feeding, and Water conditions Same as *M. lippincottianus.*
Sexing, Breeding Similar to *M. lippincottianus* except that some 2000 nonadhesive eggs are laid. These fall to the bottom of the tank. Young hatch in 70 hours at 82°F. Young only half the size of *M. lippincottianus.*

Gymnocorymbus ternetzi
(Boulenger 1895)
Popular names Black Tetra, Blackamoor, or Petticoat Fish.
Origin Brazil, Argentina, and Bolivia.
Size 2 inches.
Appearance A pert fish with large black dorsal and anal fins giving it a fanlike appearance. In well-marked specimens the posterior half of the fish, excluding the caudal fin, is jet black. Two vertical black bars adorn the silvery flank. A truly unique, deservedly popular aquarium fish. Unfortunately becomes a bit drab when over 1¼ inch long.
Behavior Inclined to some fin-nipping. Nevertheless a good community fish.
Feeding All foods, including dried foods.
Water conditions Not critical. Does

better at 68 °F. to 70 °F. rather than at the usual 80 °F. Black pigmentation best developed when kept at cooler temperature.

Sexing, Breeding Males slightly longer, females slightly deeper. In mature specimens the fuller shape of the female is unmistakable. Can be bred in near neutral water of moderate hardness; 100 to 200 adhesive eggs are laid, which hatch in 24 hours. Fry free-swimming in about three days. They need infusoria as first food.

Pristella maxillaris (Ulrey 1894)

Popular name X-ray Fish, Water Goldfinch, or Pristella
Origin Northern South America.
Size 1½ inches.

Appearance Translucent body of the fish gives it its popular name. This is not a very colorful fish; nevertheless, it is interestingly marked and is a great old-time favorite.
Behavior Very peaceful. Ideal for community tank.
Feeding Eats all foods.
Water conditions Temperature 72 °F. to 78 °F. pH and hardness not critical.
Sexing The fuller form of the female and the flat, at times concave contour of the male makes sexing easy. Black spot on anal completely crosses the fin in the female but only partially in the male.
Breeding One of the easiest Characins to breed, once a good pair has been found. Lays 400 to 500 eggs which

hatch within 24 hours. Fry very hardy and easy to rear.

Hemigrammus erythrozonus
   (Durbin 1909)
Popular name Glowlight Tetra. Before 1955 this fish was mistaken for *Hyphessobrycon gracilis*. It has also been called *Hemigrammus gracilis*.
Origin British Guiana.
Size 1¾ inches.
Appearance The most attractive feature is the glowing ruby-red line which runs along the length of this fish. In certain strains and in fish kept under unfavorable conditions this line is pale amber.
Behavior Peaceful community fish.
Feeding Eats all foods.
Water conditions Peat water heightens coloration. Temperature 78 °F.-80 °F. Seen at best when a group is kept on its own in a thickly planted tank with a dark background.
Sexing Females are larger and more robust looking. Belly contour convex. Males are slenderer and the belly is flat or even concave.
Breeding Considered to be only a little less difficult to breed than the Neon Tetra. Either the acriflavine adsorption method or the peat water method should be tried (see above, Characins). If they spawn they lay 200 to 400 eggs. The young hatch in 24 hours. If conditions are suitable one can expect to rear most of them. However, to rear anything over 50 from spawning is considered pretty good going.

Hemigrammus rhodostomus
  (Ahl 1924)
Popular name Red or Rummy Nosed Tetra.
Origin Amazon.
Size 2 inches.
Appearance A beautifully marked fish with a bright red snout.
Behavior Very hardy and peaceful.
Feeding Eats all foods.
Water conditions Moderately soft slightly acid water. 78°F.
Sexing Males smaller and slenderer than females. Nose a little more red.
Breeding One of the more difficult-to-breed Characins. Methods similar to those recommended for Glowlight have proved moderately successful.

Hyphessobrycon flammeus
  (Myers 1924)
Popular name Tetra von Rio, or Flame Tetra.
Origin Neighborhood of Rio de Janeiro.
Size 1½ inches.
Appearance A short fish. Posterior half of the body and fins gleaming red.
Behavior A hardy old favorite. Good community fish.
Feeding Accepts all foods including dried foods.
Water conditions Not critical.
Sexing Males smaller, slimmer, and more colorful. Anal fin of male shows a black edge.
Breeding Easy to breed, and will breed freely in most waters; 100 to 200 eggs laid, which hatch in 24 hours.

Paracheirodon innesi (Myers 1936)
Popular name Neon Tetra.
Origin Peru, Brazil.
Size 1¼ inches.
Appearance Widely accepted as one of the most beautiful of aquarium fishes. The iridescent greenish-blue strip and the deep red band have an intensity rarely matched in other species.
Behavior This is a rather hardy fish, well able to look after itself even in company of fishes twice its size. An ideal community fish which usually swims in the lower half of the tank.
Feeding Takes all foods.
Sexing The females are unmistakably larger and fatter than the male, the belly of which is flat or slightly sunken.
Breeding This is considered to be a difficult feat. Suitable methods have already been described earlier (see above).

Hyphessobrycon pulchripinnis
  (E. Ahl 1937)
Popular name Lemon Tetra. At one time called *Hemigrammus erythrophthalmus.*
Origin Amazon.
Size 1¾ inches.
Appearance This fish is outstanding because of the pale lemon-tinted body and the bright red color in the upper part of the eye.
Behavior A peaceful community fish.
Feeding Accepts all foods.
Water conditions Moderately soft, slightly acid water. Temperature 80°F.

Sexing Male slightly slimmer and more colorful.
Breeding Not very easy. Peat water method should be employed.

Astyanax fasciatus mexicanus
  (de Philippi 1853)
Popular name Blind Cave Tetra.
Origin Subterranean streams and pools in Mexico.
Size 2¾ inches.
Appearance A silvery rose-tinted fish. Vestigial eyes and orbits overgrown with skin. These fish are derived from *Astyanax fasciatus mexicanus* which have normal eyes. It is believed that a long time ago these fish were carried by currents into subterranean streams and the eyes atrophied and became useless.
Behavior Blindness does not present a serious handicap to this fish. It can be kept in a community tank with other fishes. A heightened sense of smell and vibration enables the fish to find its food and avoid bumping into other fishes.
Water conditions Can be kept and bred in moderately soft or moderately hard, nearly neutral waters. Temperature 78°F.
Sexing Shape is the only guide. Males are distinctly slimmer than females.
Breeding This is easy with large mature specimens; 400 to 800 semiadhesive eggs are laid, which hatch in 36 hours. Fry have small eyes, which are probably functional. They can be reared in the usual manner, commencing with infusoria as first food.

Corynopoma riisei (Gill 1858)
Popular name Swordtail Characin.
Origin Trinidad, Colombia, Venezuela.
Size 2½ inches.
Appearance A cream-colored fish with rather long translucent fins.
Behavior, Feeding An undemanding peaceful species of interesting breeding behavior. Will take dried foods but needs a reasonable amount of live or fresh foods.
Sexing The male has a peculiar, long, oarlike or spoonlike extrusion from the gill cover which extends halfway down the body. Its fins are longer and the lower lobe of the caudal is elongated. Hence the popular name Swordtail Characin.

Captions for color photos
Spawning pair of tiger barbs, Capoeta tetrazona; *p. 17. A large school of cardinal tetras,* Paracheirodon axelrodi, *is one of the most colorful sights to be found in the freshwater aquarium; photo by Dr. Herbert R. Axelrod; p. 18.* Tanichthys albonubes, *the White Cloud Mountain minnow; photo by Dr. Herbert R. Axelrod; p. 19. Spawning pair of* Nothobranchius palmquisti, *an African annual killifish; photo by H. J. Richter; p. 20. A blushing angel (in foreground) spawning with a more normal color variety of angelfish,* Pterophyllum scalare; *photo by H. J. Richter; p. 21. The brilliant color and flowing fins are typical of males of many modern varieties of the guppy,* Poecilia reticulata; *photo by H. J. Richter; p. 22. The sailfin molly,* Poecilia latipinna; *p. 23. The black ruby barb of Ceylon,* Puntius nigrofasciatus; *photo by H. J. Richter; p. 24.*

Breeding This is fairly easy but what happens during the mating act is as yet uncertain. The male approaches the female and extends his gill appendages so that they stand off at right angles to the body. The female sometimes turns around to snap at one of them. It is believed that at this stage the male somehow transfers a package of sperms (spermatophores) into the oviduct of the female. Once the female is fertilized in this fashion she will go on delivering fertile eggs for many months or even the rest of her life without further assistance from the male. This is a fairly easy fish to breed and is not critical of water requirements. About 100 eggs are laid and the female looks after them and transfers them from leaf to leaf. The male should be removed after spawning, the female when the fry become free-swimming.

Paracheirodon axelrodi
(Schultz 1956)
Popular name Cardinal Tetra.
Origin Upper Rio Negro, Brazil, and Colombia.
Size 1¾ inches.
Appearance This fish resembles the Neon Tetra (*Paracheirodon innesi*). It differs from it by being somewhat larger and more colorful, for whereas the red band in the Neon extends from the tail to the middle of the body, in the Cardinal it carries on to the gill covers.
Behavior, Feeding, Water conditions, Sexing, Breeding Same as for Neon Tetra.

Copella arnoldi (Regan 1912)
Popular name Spraying Characin.
Origin Venezuela, Brazil, Guiana.
Size 3 inches.
Appearance An elegantly shaped slender fish with elongated fins.
Feeding Accepts all foods.
Water conditions Moderately soft neutral water.
Sexing The male has longer fins and there is a white spot at the root of its dorsal fin.
Breeding This fish is kept mainly because of its unusual breeding habit. It spawns outside water, e.g., on the surface of an overhanging leaf or on the undersurface of the aquarium cover glass. The conditioned pair are introduced in a 10- to 15-gallon, sparsely planted tank with the water level lying about 1″ to 1½″ below the cover glass. The pair swim side by side and together jump out of the water to the undersurface of the cover glass, where they adhere for a moment, deposit 10 to 15 eggs, and fall back into the tank. This act is repeated until some 100 eggs are laid. When spawning is completed the female should be removed. The male looks after the eggs and prevents them from drying by splashing them with water. This process sometimes dislodges the eggs or newly hatched fry which, when they fall into the water, are devoured by the male. If this is seen to happen, the male should be removed and an aerator stone fixed in the tank so that the spray from the bursting bubbles keeps the eggs damp.

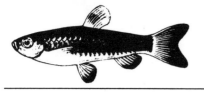 

By about the fourth day the fry drop into the water and swim about freely. Just before this happens it is best to remove the male and rear the fry in the usual way.

Copeina guttata (Steindachner 1875)
Popular name Redspotted Copeina.
Origin Central Amazon.
Size 4 inches. Aquarium specimens up to 5 inches.
Appearance Not as elegant or streamlined as *C. arnoldi.* It has a bluish silvery body and yellowish fins with orange-red margins.
Behavior Reasonably peaceful, but it is rather large for the average community collection.
Feeding, Water conditions Same as *C. arnoldi.*
Sexing The male is more colorful than the female. It also shows rows of tiny red dots on the flank. Few or no such dots occur on the female.
Breeding This is another Characin with an unusual breeding habit. It lays its eggs in depressions in the gravel or on a flat stone. The male fans the eggs and looks after them. The breeding procedure is reminiscent of Cichlids and Sunfishes rather than Characins. About 200 to 300 eggs are laid, which hatch in 2 days. The female should be removed after spawning and the male soon after the fry become free-swimming.

Anostomidae

These Central and South American fishes are often very beautifully marked but unfortunately most of them are a bit too large for the usual community aquarium. Many of them have a habit of drifting about with the head down and aquarists therefore call them Headstanders.

Anostomus anostomus
    (Linnaeus 1758)
Popular name Striped Anostomus.
Origin South America.
Size 6 inches.
Appearance A rather startling fish with a long cylindrical body and pointed snout. The body is traversed by longitudinal strips of black and gold; a red spot on the root of the caudal fin which leaves the lobes colorless completes the bizarre color combination.
Behavior Swims in a head-down fashion but straightens up when it darts forward. Can be kept in company with other large fishes.
Feeding Mainly live and frozen foods supplemented with green foods such as lettuce.
Water conditions Not critical. Temperature 78 °F.
Sexing, Breeding Not known.

Chilodus punctatus (Muller and Troschel 1844)
Popular name Pearl Headstander or Spotted Headstander
Origin Northern South America.
Size 3½ inches.
Appearance The elongated grayish-green body is covered by rows of brown

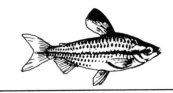

spots. The fish swims head down at an angle of 45° from the horizontal.

Behavior Very peaceful; can be kept in community aquaria.

Feeding Eats all foods but must be provided with fresh green foods such as lettuce and spinach.

Water conditions Moderately soft, slightly acid water. Temperature 80°F.

Sexing Females plumper than males.

Breeding Has been seldom bred. Method same as that described for other Characins. About 150 to 200 brownish eggs are laid. Fry difficult to rear.

Lebiasinidae

The Lebiasinidae resemble the Characins in many respects but differ from them in that in most of them the lower jaw is toothless. Some of the smallest and prettiest aquarium fishes belong to this family. They come from South America. Most of them have a thin elongated body and are popularly called Pencilfishes. The scientific nomenclature of the fishes in this family is truly chaotic.

The genus *Nannostomus* was described by Gunther in 1872. In 1909 Eigenmann removed one of the fishes from this genus and established a new genus called *Poecilobrycon* for it. This was done on the basis of differences in the adipose fin. Some subsequent workers have accepted this and placed other fishes in the genus *Poecilobrycon*; others, however, have refused to accept the genus *Poecilobrycon* on the ground that these differences are neither constant nor clear-cut. To add to the difficulty, fishes of the genus *Nannostomus* show remarkable changes of color pattern during their life and even during a single day.

Nannostomus beckfordi

(Gunther 1872)

Popular name Beckford's Pencilfish, or Golden Pencilfish

Origin Amazon Basin. British Guiana.

Size 1¾ inches.

Appearance The elongated body has a golden-brown tint and is traversed by a longitudinal black band edged with gold and sometimes with red. At night the horizontal band fades and dark bands or blotches appear on the sides.

Behavior A peaceful fish suitable for the community tank; hardy in spite of its delicate appearance.

Water conditions Moderately soft to moderately hard, near neutral to slightly acidic water. Temperature 80°F.

Sexing The plump shape of the female is the main guide. The male is slightly more colorful. Red coloration in fins and on the body is almost exclusive to the male.

Breeding This is one of the easiest aquarium fishes to breed. It does not destroy its eggs or young. It can be bred in the usual Characin fashion but the number of young produced is likely to be small. A simpler method is to place three or four females with two males in a well-planted tank or a tank containing

a fair amount of some artifical spawning medium, and feed them well. The tank will soon be seen to contain many (50 to 100) young fry in various stages of development. Either the adults can now be moved to a fresh tank or the fry ladled out and reared elsewhere.

Nannostomus eques
(Steindachner 1876)
(also called *Poecilobrycon* or *Nannobrycon eques*).
Popular name Tube Mouthed Pencilfish or Brown-Tailed Pencilfish
Origin Amazon.
Size 2 inches.
Appearance Another Pencilfish which swims at an angle. It has an elongated snout.
Behavior A peaceful fish.
Feeding, Water conditions Same as other *Nannostomus* species.
Sexing Males slimmer than females.
Breeding Usual Characin method but seem to prefer spawning on broad-leaved plants such as *Hygrophila* and *Ludwigia*.

Nannostomus marginatus
(Eigenmann 1909)
Popular name Dwarf Pencilfish.
Origin West Guiana.
Size 1¼ inches.
Appearance This is the smallest *Nannostomus*. It is rather more stocky than others. A pretty black-banded fish with splashes of red in the fins.
Behavior Very peaceful, rather shy. Best kept with other small fishes.

Feeding, Water conditions Same as for *N. anomalus.*
Sexing The males are brighter in color than females.
Breeding Eats its own eggs so cannot be bred like *N. anomalus,* but can be bred like other Characins; 25 to 75 eggs laid at a spawning which hatch in 2 days. However, the same pair can spawn again in three or four days.

Nannostomus unifasciatus
(Steindachner 1876)
Popular name Tail-eyed Pencilfish or One-Lined Pencilfish
Origin Guiana, Amazon.
Size 2 inches.
Appearance One of the handsomest Pencilfishes. It swims head up at an angle of 30° to the horizontal. The lower lobe of the caudal fin is enlarged and carries a large, colorful spot.
Behavior A peaceful fish suitable for the community tank.
Feeding, Water conditions Similar to other *Nannostomus* species.
Sexing, Breeding Males slimmer than females. Have been bred occasionally but reports are scanty and inconclusive.

Nannostomus trifasciatus
(Steindachner 1876)
Popular name Three Banded Pencilfish.
Origin West Guiana, Amazon.
Size 1½ inches.
Appearance Universally accepted as the prettiest *Nannostomus*, but unfortunately rather rare. As its name implies, it has three black lines running

along a gold-colored body. Numerous vivid red marks on the body and fins.
Behavior   Peaceful community fish.
Feeding, Water conditions   Same as other *Nannostomus* species.
Sexing   Difficult. Female slightly paler and plumper.
Breeding   Difficult to breed. It is said that they can be induced to spawn in plant thickets in peaty water of pH 6.5 and hardness 60 ppm. Only 30 to 70 eggs are laid. Fry difficult to rear.

Gasteropelecidae (Hatchetfishes)

These markedly compressed, extremely deep-bodied fishes come mainly from northern South America. Some species are capable of rapidly flapping their pectoral fins and are probably the only true "flying fishes." They can jump out of the water and "fly" or glide some 10 to 15 feet.

Carnegiella marthae (Myers 1927)
Popular name   Blackwinged Hatchetfish.
Origin   Venezuela, Peru, Amazon, Rio Negro, Orinoco.
Size   1¼ inches.
Appearance   A small and delicate species. The middle portions of the pectorals are black; so is the keel.
Behavior   A small, peaceful fish, best kept with others of its own kind.
Feeding   Accepts all foods.
Water conditions   Very soft, slightly acid water.
Sexing, Breeding   Not much is known

about this; they have been bred occasionally. Method recommended is similar to that employed for *Hyphessobrycon* species.

Gasteropelecus levis
   (Eigenmann 1909)
Popular name   Silver Hatchetfish (Giant).
Origin   Lower Amazon.
Size   2½ inches.
Appearance   This is a silvery fish with a single slim blue-black horizontal band.
Behavior   Perhaps the most robust of all the Hatchetfishes available to the aquarist; does fairly well in a community tank, if given good conditions.
Feeding, Water conditions   Same as for other Hatchetfishes.
Sexing, Breeding   Not known. Has not been bred in captivity.

Family Cyprinidae (Carps and Carplike Fishes)

This, the largest family of bony fishes, is widely distributed in Asia, Africa, Europe, and North America. Carps do not occur naturally in Northern Canada, South America, Australia, New Zealand, or Madagascar.

Most of them have the classical fish shape: not too compressed body, with a convex dorsal and ventral profile. Carps do not have teeth in the mouth but they have pharyngeal bones surmounted by grinding teeth. No Carp has an adipose

fin. Some of them have one or two pairs of barbels. The largest Carp grows to about 8 ft. in length (*Barbus tor*, one of the Indian Mahseers) but there are many that are small and suitable for the aquarium. Of the aquarium Carps, a number (like the Goldfish) are cold water fishes and do not concern us here.

Brachydanio albolineatus
  (Blyth 1860)
Popular name Pearl Danio, or Gold Danio.
Origin India and Sumatra.
Size 2 inches.
Appearance Slim, moderately compressed, iridescent body. Mother-of-pearl appearance when viewed by reflected light. Different strains have been developed, some showing predominantly red and yellow iridescence, others green and blue iridescence.
Behavior A peaceful schooling fish which makes a good community inhabitant. For a spectacular display a number of these should be housed in a well-planted tank with dark gravel at the bottom. Light should be arranged so that it strikes the fish from the front.
Feeding, Water conditions As for *Brachydanio rerio*.
Sexing Males more colorful and slimmer than females.
Breeding Same as for *B. rerio*.

Brachydanio nigrofasciatus
  (Day 1869)
Popular name Spotted Danio.

Origin Burma, India.
Size 1½ inches.
Appearance Similar in shape and appearance to *B. rerio* except that it has fewer stripes and some spots on its sides.
Behavior, Feeding, Water conditions, Sexing, Breeding Same as for *B. rerio* except that it is a bit more difficult to induce spawning.

Brachydanio rerio
  (Hamilton-Buchanan 1822)
Popular name Zebra Danio.
Origin Eastern part of India.
Size 1¾ inches.
Appearance Slim, almost cylindrical body with attractive bluish black and silvery or golden stripes.
Behavior A peaceful schooling fish which contributes much to the community tank by its constant, but not restless, movement.
Feeding Accepts all food.
Water conditions Not critical.
Sexing Females obviously plumper. Mature males have a yellowish cast, the bands appearing golden rather than silver.
Breeding Considered to be one of the easiest fishes to breed. Lays nonadhesive eggs, which fall to the bottom of the tank; avid spawn eaters, hence the eggs must be protected. One of the simplest ways of breeding this fish is to cover the bottom of the tank with a 1 inch layer of pebbles (½ inch diam.). A few fine-leaved plants or nylon mops may or may not be introduced. Water depth not

more than 3 inches for the fish eat many eggs as they fall slowly through the water. It is generally recommended that a long tank should be used so as to allow these fish chasing room during spawning. It is not absolutely necessary, for personal experience has shown that they will spawn equally readily in a goldfish globe with nothing more than a few pebbles at the bottom. For large-scale breeding, trays with a plastic mesh bottom can be employed. The mesh size should be such that the eggs but not the fish can pass through. Half a dozen or more fish can be placed in the trays at a time. When spawning is complete, the fish are removed. Eggs usually hatch in 2 or 3 days but at times this may be delayed to as long as 5 or 6 days, even when the temperature is held at 80°F. The fry need infusoria as first food. They are easily reared, for they can be given substantial quantities of dried foods from an early age.

Danio aequipinnatus
(McClelland 1839)
Popular name Giant Danio.
Origin Ceylon, West coast of India (Malabar).
Size Up to 4 inches.
Appearance A silvery fish with blue and yellow longitudinal stripes. When in breeding condition most of the fins show a reddish hue.
Behavior Peaceful—can be kept in company of larger fishes. A restless swimmer difficult to net.
Feeding Huge appetite. Eats all foods.

Water conditions Not critical. A species that does reasonably well in moderate to fairly hard neutral or alkaline water; lives best in a large long tank with plenty of swimming space. Temperature 80°F.
Sexing Specimens over 2½ inch in length can be sexed by the fuller shape of the female. The blue and yellow bands are more interrupted in the male. Reddish hue in the fins is more marked in male.
Breeding A fairly large tank (10 to 15 gallons) with a 1 inch layer of pebbles on the bottom and some nylon mops or fine-leaved plants should be prepared and the conditioned pair introduced; 200 to 300 semiadhesive eggs are laid. Fry hatch in 3 days and become free-swimming on the 6th day.

Labeo bicolor (Smith 1931)
Popular name Redtailed Black Shark.
Origin Thailand.
Size 4½ inches.
Appearance As its popular name implies, this fish has the torpedo-shaped body and flaglike dorsal of a shark. The body is velvety black and the tail crimson red in the good specimens. Yellow or orange caudal fin indicates unsuitable aquarium conditions or a poor strain of fish.
Behavior An excellent fish for the community tank. Its large sucker-like mouth helps to keep plants and front glass clean. Of peaceful temperament, but bullies smaller members of its own kind.

Feeding A scavenger. Eats all foods, including algae.

Water conditions Not critical. Some authorities advocate hard alkaline water, others soft acid water.

Sexing, Breeding Has been bred but no details available.

Tanichthys albonubes (Lin 1932)

Popular name White Cloud Mountain Minnow.

Origin China, Canton, from the rivers of the White Cloud Mountains.

Size 1¼ inches.

Appearance An olive-brown fish with a bright golden longitudinal band extending from snout to root of caudal peduncle. Yellow and red markings in dorsal and caudal fins.

Behavior Peaceful community fish.

Feeding Eats all foods.

Water conditions Near neutral water of moderate hardness. Temperature 50°F.-75°F. Thrives at about 70°F.

Sexing Males noticeably slimmer than females.

Breeding This fish breeds like the *Brachydanios,* laying nonadhesive eggs. If fed well, most pairs do not molest eggs or fry. If a few fish are kept in a planted tank, numerous babies will be soon found.

Barbs

This group provides an unusually large number of very popular aquarium fishes. Most Barbs are gay, colorful, active fishes, easy to feed, not choosy about water conditions, and breed readily. It is useful to divide aquarium Barbs into two groups, small Barbs which grow to 2 or 3 inches in size and large Barbs that grow to larger sizes.

The small Barbs are ideal community fishes; the larger ones can be a nuisance for they are likely to stir up the mulm, uproot plants, and generally behave like a bull in a china shop. However, the larger Barbs, too, are attractive fishes. As a rule the smaller fry of the small Barbs need infusoria as first food. The fry of larger Barbs can usually manage brine shrimps.

Barbs thrive in mature well-oxygenated water with plenty of swimming space. In an overcrowded tank they are usually the first to show distress.

Most Barbs lay adhesive or semiadhesive eggs; hence they can be spawned by the methods described under Characins. Briefly, this consists of providing a fairly well-planted tank with pebbles on the bottom. They can also be spawned on nylon or willow root. Barbs are avid spawn eaters and should be removed immediately spawning is completed.

Puntius conchonius

(Hamilton-Buchanan 1822)

Popular name Rosy Barb, or Red Barb.

Origin India.

Size 2½ inches.

Appearance One of the prettiest Barbs when in good condition. Basically, this

is a silvery fish which becomes suffused with a deep rosy red or pale green tint when conditions suit it. The fins show a variable amount of black pigmentation.
Behavior Peaceful but rather boisterous. Should not be kept with very small fishes.
Feeding Hearty appetite. Eats all foods.
Water condition Near neutral to slightly alkaline, moderately hard to hard water. Temperature 78 °F.
Sexing When in color the rosy hue of the male contrasts with the predominantly yellowish-green of the female. Tip of dorsal fin in male is black. In female this area shows a dark tint; all her other fins are clear.
Breeding One of the easiest egg layers to breed. Beginners could start with this one. The eggs are adhesive; 200 to 300 are produced at a spawning. Method of breeding as described earlier.

Puntius nigrofasciatus (Gunther 1868)
Popular name Black Ruby, or Purple-headed Barb.
Origin Ceylon.
Size 2½ inches.
Appearance The female is a yellowish-gray fish with three to four dark vertical bands or blotches. The male is brownish black to black and the anterior part of the fish is vermilion-red.
Behavior An attractive and popular community fish.
Feeding Accepts all foods.
Water conditions Not critical, but shows off best in near neutral water of

moderate hardness.
Sexing As described above.
Breeding Another easily bred Barb; it lays 200 to 300 eggs. Method same as for other Barbs.

Capoeta tetrazona (Bleeker 1855)
Popular name Tiger Barb, or Sumatra Barb.
Origin Sumatra, Borneo.
Size 2 inches.
Appearance Reddish-yellow fish with four broad black evenly spaced bands.
Behavior Variable. Some aquarists find this a peaceful community fish. Others complain that it is a bully and fin nipper. Nevertheless it is widely held to be one of the prettiest community fishes.
Feeding, Water conditions Same as other Barbs.
Sexing The slimmer, more colorful males are easily picked out from the plainer, plumper females. There is more red in all the fins of the male. The author has noticed that very young fish can be sexed by studying the distribution of red pigment in the ventral fins. In the female the red pigment is concentrated at the root of the fin while the free edge is transparent and colorless. In the male the entire fin is red and the pigment is more concentrated in the free edge.
Breeding Same as other Barbs. Fry susceptible to fin rot and swim bladder trouble. Telescope-eyed mutants (similar to those in Goldfish) are sometimes encountered. Extremely clean conditions

must be maintained when rearing the young.

Capoeta titteya (Deraniyagala 1929)
Popular name Cherry Barb.
Origin Ceylon.
Size 2 inches.
Appearance Yellowish-brown or reddish-brown fish with dark longitudinal black band.
Behavior An ideal community fish.
Feeding, Water conditions Same as other Barbs.
Sexing The male is darker. At breeding time it turns cherry red and the black band disappears almost completely. The female is noticeably plumper and lighter colored.
Breeding Same as other Barbs; it lays 100 to 200 eggs. Some pairs are avid egg eaters. Others leave both eggs and fry alone.

Rasbora heteromorpha
  (Duncker 1904)
Popular name (Red) Rasbora, or Harlequin Fish.
Origin Malaya, Sumatra, Thailand.
Size 1¾ inches.
Appearance This is an old favorite. The large wedge-shaped blue-black area is set on a violet- and rose-pink-shaded body.
Behavior A schooling fish of great beauty, which deserves to be given a tank to itself. It is also suitable as a community fish.
Feeding Accepts all foods.
Water conditions Soft, slightly acid,

peaty water. Temperature 80°F.
Sexing Mature males are slimmer and have more red in dorsal and caudal fin. Sexing by extent of wedge-shaped blotch is unreliable.
Breeding This is a difficult fish to breed. A well-conditioned pair should be placed in a tank containing peaty water (pH 6.2, hardness under 40 ppm) and some *Cryptocoryne*. The pair usually spawn up-side-down on the under surface of the leaf. It is said that not every male will breed with every female so if no spawning is obtained one of the partners should be substituted. Usually less than 100 eggs are laid, which hatch in 24 hours.

Cobitidae

This family provides some quaint but useful scavengers and algae eaters.

The Cobitidae come from the old world, and like the Carps they have no teeth in their jaws. They have three or more pairs of barbels. Some members of the family, the spiny Loaches, have a simple or bifid spine just under each eye. Normally this lies folded flat, but if threatened it is erected with the result that any predator attempting to swallow it receives an unpleasant surprise.

These fishes are scavengers that live at the bottom of the pond in muddy, poorly oxygenated water. To compensate for this some species come to the surface and swallow air. They carry on a form of intestinal respiration,

extracting oxygen via the mucosa of the hind gut. The spent air is expelled through the vent. Some Loaches are believed to be sensitive to changes in atmospheric pressure (Weather Fish).

Acanthophthalmus semicinctus
(Fraser-Brunner 1940)

Popular name   Half Banded Coolie Loach.
Origin   East Indies.
Size   3½ inches.
Appearance   Many fishes with a tubular snakelike body covered by black and yellow markings are offered to the aquarist. Some are distinct species, others are subspecies of *A. kuhlii*. The fish we are considering has a salmon-pink belly and the black and yellow markings extend only halfway round the fish.
Behavior   A peaceful fish that is often kept in community tanks. Since it is of nocturnal habit and hides at the bottom, it is rarely seen by its owner. The best way is to keep a collection of these Loaches in a small, sparsely planted tank with some peat on the bottom and many hiding places; then one can study their interesting behavior.
Feeding   All food, particularly algae and *Tubifex*.
Water conditions   Not critical; near neutral, moderately hard water at 78°F.
Sexing   The females become noticeably plumper at spawning time.
Breeding   Not much is known about this. When these fishes are kept on their own as described above, small Loaches

appear. If this is seen adults should be removed to another tank and the young reared in the usual way.

Botia macracantha (Bleeker 1852)

Popular name   Clown Loach, or Tiger Botia.
Origin   Sumatra, Borneo.
Size   4½ inches.
Appearance   The color pattern of this *Botia* bears an amazing resemblance to a Tiger Barb *(Capoeta tetrazona)*. The body is golden-yellow with three dark blue-black bands.
Behavior   A peaceful community fish. A fairly good scavenger. Does not like strong light. Should have hiding places.
Water conditions   Most *Botias* prefer alkaline, moderately hard to hard water. This one is fairly tolerant regarding water requirements but the other extreme of soft acid water must be avoided. Temperature 70°F.-75°F.
Sexing, Breeding   Not bred in captivity.

Siluridae

This family contains Asiatic and European Catfishes with a naked skin. Eyes are usually covered by a transparent layer of skin. Adipose fin absent. Only a few species are of interest to aquarists.

Kryptopterus bicirrhis
(Cuvier and Valenciennes 1839)

Popular name   Glass Catfish.
Origin   India, Greater Sunda Islands.
Size   3½ inches.

Appearance Strongly compressed transparent glasslike body with a long-based anal fin, which is continually undulated by the fish. A pair of long maxillary barbels (whiskers).

Behavior Can be kept in a community tank but it is inclined to lurk at the back of the tank, standing in one spot undulating its anal fin. An interesting fish best kept with its own kind.

Feeding Mainly live foods; will not pick up food from bottom but will take dried food as it descends in the tank.

Water conditions Not critical.

Sexing, Breeding Not bred in captivity.

Mochokidae

This family contains naked Catfishes from Africa. Adipose fin present.

Synodontis nigriventris (David 1936)

Popular name Upside-down Catfish.

Origin Belgian Congo.

Size 2 inches.

Appearance Body shape similar to *Corydoras*. Ventral surface dark. This represents a reversal of normal obliterative coloring of fishes that have a dark dorsal surface and a light ventral surface.

Behavior Kept mainly for its interesting habit of swimming upside down. Peaceful community fish.

Feeding Live foods and algae, which it obtains from undersurface of leaves.

Water conditions Not critical.

Sexing, Breeding Not known. Has spawned inside a flowerpot.

Malapteruridae

There is only one species in this family.

Malapterurus electricus
(Gmelin 1789)

Popular name Electric Catfish.

Origin In some lakes and rivers of central and west Africa.

Size 2 feet, aquarium specimens 10 inches.

Appearance Long, almost cylindrical body. It has a large adipose fin but the dorsal fin is absent. Small phosphorescent eyes. The main interest lies in the electric organs.

Behavior Has to be kept in solitary confinement. Can give a considerable shock if disturbed or touched. The discharge is weaker than that produced by the electric eel (*Electrophorus electricus*) but stronger than that produced by the Mormyridae. It is not clear whether the electric organ is used to stun and catch smaller fishes or whether it serves as a kind of sonar.

Feeding A voracious nocturnal feeder. Eats earthworms, meat, and smaller fishes.

Water conditions Not critical.

Sexing, Breeding Not accomplished in captivity.

Callichthyidae (Armored Catfishes, Mailed Catfishes)

This family contains the mailed or armored Catfishes of South America

and Trinidad. The flanks are covered by a double series of overlapping bony plates; the head and back are also similarly covered in some species. The adipose fin is supported by a mobile spine, and a large spine also occurs in the dorsal fin. With such protection it is not surprising that even large fishes leave them strictly alone. The mouth is small and toothless and is surmounted by one or two pairs of barbels. The eyes have a limited movement in their sockets, a fact which adds considerably to their droll appearance. Like the Cobitidae, these fishes are adapted for intestinal respiration. The swim bladder occurs in two parts and is surrounded by a bony capsule.

Genus Corydoras

The family Callichthyidae contains the genus *Corydoras*, a most charming and popular group of small Catfishes suitable for the aquarium. Not only are they hardy, inquisitive, droll creatures interesting in their own right but they also perform a useful sanitary function by going over the aquarium floor and disposing of food left by other fishes, which might otherwise cause pollution.

Although a number of them have been bred occasionally, they are somewhat difficult to induce to spawn. This is perhaps because most aquarists keep them as scavengers and not as interesting fish in their own right, whose dietetic and other needs are studied and provided for. For breeding *Corydoras* it is best to give a group of these fishes a tank to themselves, and feed them well. A large part of the diet should be comprised of various worms and a fair amount of other usual fresh foods. The sexes are not hard to distinguish in many *Corydoras*, for when viewed from above the female will be seen to be much broader and fuller than the male. Often the fins of the male tend to be longer and somewhat more pointed than those of the female.

The tank should be provided with a fairly dark-colored fine gravel bottom. It should be lightly planted with *Cryptocoryne* and provided with hiding places, such as broken flowerpots or stones arranged to form arches and tunnels. Temperature should not be too high for most species like cooler conditions (around 72°F.) than other tropicals, and strong light should be avoided. It is generally accepted that most *Corydoras* do best in neutral to slightly alkaline water of moderate hardness. As the fishes mature and the sexes become distinguishable, another tank should be set up similar to the one already described so that the sexes can be segregated and conditioned.

As mating time approaches there is a heightening of their colors. Some species take on a pale rosy hue. It is now time to set up a spawning tank of about 10- to 15-gallon capacity, in the same way as the main tanks. The chosen pair is now introduced and should spawn in a day or two. If they

fail to do so try dropping the temperature to 62°F. by adding fresh cold water. This sometimes brings on the spawning urge. If the pair have not spawned within a week try another pair, or try one female with two or three males.

The premating behavior of the *Corydoras* is worth watching. The male continually nudges the excited female, who swims restlessly all over the tank; often the male swims over the female's back. The male then lies on his back or side or rises slightly so as to present his ventral surface to the female. What happens now is not at all clear. Some maintain that the female collects the sperm in her mouth by sucking it out of the male's genital papilla; others believe that at this point she extrudes some eggs, which stick to her ventral fin, and that these are fertilized by the sperm liberated by the male and brought to her ventral fin by the movement of her fins and gill cover. When the embrace is over the female swims away, cleans a spot on the glass wall of the tank or a leaf, and deposits her eggs. Those who maintain that the female carries the sperm in her mouth believe that the cleaning act prior to deposition of the eggs is in fact concerned with spitting out the collected sperm prior to deposition of the eggs.

After numerous embraces some 200-400 eggs are laid. These are very large (2 mm.) and clear at first but become amber-colored later. Many eggs are usually infertile or do not hatch for

other reasons; they go chalky white. The fish, once they have spawned, should be removed; even though they are not avid spawn eaters they have no further duties to perform and are best out of the way. In order to prevent too much fungus growth and bacterial activity from the rotten eggs it is best to tint the water a light blue with some methylene blue. It takes about six days for the eggs to hatch. The young are large and easily reared on brine shrimps, with microworms as first food.

Corydoras aeneus (Gill 1858)
Popular name Bronze Corydoras.
Origin Trinidad, Venezuela.
Size 2½ inches.
Appearance One of the hardiest and most popular of aquarium Catfishes. It has a greenish flank and a pinkish body.
Behavior A perfect community fish. Very peaceful—will not molest even very tiny fishes.
Feeding Eats dried food that falls to the bottom. Loves whiteworms and *Tubifex*.
Water conditions Neutral to alkaline, moderately hard water. Intolerant of salt (NaCl) in water.
Sexing, Breeding As described earlier for *Corydoras*.

Corydoras julii (Steindachner 1906)
Popular name Leopard Corydoras.
Origin Tributaries of the Lower Amazon.
Size 2½ inches.
Appearance Probably the most

attractively marked *Corydoras*. The silver-gray body is traversed by a longitudinal stripe and numerous dark spots.
Behavior Typical peaceful *Corydoras*.
Feeding, Water conditions, Sexing, Breeding As for other *Corydoras*.

Corydoras melanistius (Regan 1912)
Popular name Black-spotted Corydoras.
Origin Guiana, Venezuela.
Size 2½ inches.
Appearance Silver-gray body covered with evenly placed small black dots. Wedge-shaped blotch on nape of neck entending to dorsal fin. Black band across eye and head.
Behavior, Water conditions, Feeding, Sexing, Breeding As described earlier for other *Corydoras*.

Corydoras paleatus (Jenyns 1842)
Popular name Peppered Corydoras.
Origin Brazil and La Plata Basin.
Size 2¾ inches.
Appearance Body of an olive-brown color, with dark almost black blotches. As popular and common as *C. aeneus*. An albino strain has been developed.
Behavior A peaceful community fish which loves to disport at the front part of the aquarium floor, keeping area under feeding ring tidy. Amuses onlookers by frequent movement of eye.
Feeding Dried food. *Tubifex* and white worms.
Water conditions, Sexing, Breeding As described earlier for *Corydoras*.

Loricariidae

The Loricariidae like the Callichthyidae are armored Catfishes from northern and central south America. They have three or four series of bony plates on their sides, in contrast to the Callichthyidae which have only two. The head and the dorsal (back) and ventral (under) surfaces (except the abdomen) are also protected by bony plates in most species. The first ray of all fins except the caudal is stiffened to form a spine.

The mouth is placed on the ventral (under) surface of the flattened head. These fishes are popularly known as sucking Catfishes because the mouth is surrounded by broad-lobed lips, which form a sucking disc by which they anchor themselves to objects in the aquarium. These fishes are also sometimes referred to as algae-eating Catfishes because with their rough rasp-like lips they can scrape off algae from rockwork, plants, and glass walls of the tank. The importance of this to aquarists can hardly be overstated and many consider that no decorative community tank should be without one or more fishes belonging to this family.

While no Catfish can completely eliminate the need for cleaning the front glass of the tank, members of this family do cut down the frequency with which this not too pleasant task has to be performed by the aquarist. Further, the removal of algae and debris from the leaves of aquatic plants not only

enhances their appearance but also promotes healthy condition and better growth.

Loricaria parva (Boulenger 1895)
Popular name Alligator Catfish, Whiptail Catfish.
Origin Paraguay.
Size 4½ inches.
Appearance The main interest here is in the long tapering body and the upper lobe of the caudal fin, which terminates in a long whiplike filament. It is a brownish fish with mottled black markings, which blend with the aquarium gravel.
Behavior A peaceful community fish, which would no doubt be more popular if it were freely available.
Feeding Must have plenty of algae supplemented with other green foods such as lettuce leaves. Also accepts various fresh protein foods such as shrimps or fish roe. Will also eat a little dried food.
Water conditions It comes from fast-moving water so a well-oxygenated tank is needed. Slightly acid soft to medium hard water. Happier at lower temperatures around 70°F.
Sexing, Breeding Has been accomplished on a few occasions only. The females are slightly plumper than the males. They spawn on flat stones, under arches, or in tubes about 2 inches in diameter. The male guards eggs until they hatch in just over a week. Fry reared on mashed worms, dried food, and algae.

Otocinclus affinis (Steindachner 1876)
Popular name Midget Sucker Catfish.
Origin Southeast Brazil.
Size 2 inches.
Appearance A gray-green to brown fish of not very attractive appearance.
Behavior This is the supreme algae eater for the usual community tank, which will not damage even the finest-leaved plant. One or more should be used, depending on the size of the tank. A long-lived hardy species if right conditions are provided.
Feeding Unless algae are available this fish will not survive long. Also accepts the other usual foods including dried foods.
Water conditions Not critical. Wide temperature range, does well at 78°F. and also at 65°F. for considerable periods. I have kept them in tanks housing fancy Goldfish.
Sexing Adult female markedly fatter than male.
Breeding This is similar to the *Corydoras*. Eggs are laid on the glass and on plant leaves. Young hatch in 2 or 3 days and cling to glass or plants for a similar period before they drop to the bottom searching for food. Fry reared on mashed worms, algae, and dried foods.

Cyprinodontidae (Tooth-carps)

This large family of fishes is widely distributed in the tropical and

b

subtropical region of every continent except Australia. The distinction between these fishes and the true Carps is clearly indicated by both the scientific and the popular name of this family. Carps have pharyngeal teeth but a toothless mouth. The Cyprinodontidae have both oral and pharyngeal teeth.

These fishes usually have a flattened head with an upturned mouth. No barbels or adipose fins occur.

Some of the Cyprinodontidae are egglayers, others livebearers. In the latter the anal fin is modified to form an intromittent organ called the gonopodium. So varied are the aquatic needs and methods of reproduction in this family that broad generalizations are inadequate. It is essential to consider each genus, and at times each species, separately. It should be noted that the distinction between the egg-laying and livebearing species is one of convenience. Taxonomically some of the livebearers are more closely allied to some egglaying forms than to other livebearers.

Genera Aplocheilus and Oryzias (Asiatic Tooth-carps)

The Asiatic Tooth-carps are mainly surface-living fishes that are found in fast-moving streams, ponds, and small drainage ditches. Little wonder then that they are not very demanding in their water conditions or temperature requirements. They do well in a temperature range between 70 °F. and 80 °F., in all except very hard alkaline water. In their native habitat they live on mosquito larvae and other insect life. In the aquarium too it is advisable to give them a fair amount of live and fresh meaty food, and only occasionally dried foods.

Most of the species are easily bred in small or medium-sized tanks (2 to 10 gallons) containing neutral or slightly acid peat-filtered water of moderate hardness. The tank should be furnished with limefree gravel, fine-leaved plants, and floating plants. Next the conditioned pair is introduced in the tank. They lay a few eggs each day for a period of one to three weeks, which hatch in about ten to fifteen days. In many species the eggs are at first attached to the ventral fins or ventral surface of the female and later brushed off on the floating plants. Most parents do not molest the eggs but may devour the fry when they hatch out. To prevent this three courses of action are open to the aquarist: (1) He can keep the fish in the spawning tank for a week or ten days and then move them to a fresh tank before the eggs hatch out. (2) He can remove egg-laden plants to a separate hatching tank and supply fresh plants for the fish to spawn on, or (3) He can knock off the eggs from the floating plants into the hatching tank and return the plants to the spawning tank. I prefer the first method, which is the least time-consuming.

If one is not concerned with the loss

of a few fry one can leave the pair permanently in the spawning tank and ladle out the young as they hatch out each day.

Since the "old" eggs hatch before the newly laid ones, there will be a considerable disparity of size among youngsters in a spawning. In order to prevent cannibalism it is advisable to sort out the youngsters by size occasionally.

Most of these fishes can also be spawned on nylon mops. These are best suspended in the water to imitate rootlets of floating plants. When the mop is laden with eggs either the mops or eggs are removed in the same manner as that described earlier with floating plants.

Aplocheilus blocki (Arnold 1911)
Popular name Dwarf or Green Panchax (also called Panchax Parvus).
Origin India and Ceylon.
Size 1¾ inches.
Appearance This is the smallest Panchax known to aquarists. It has a metallic greenish-yellow body with rows of red and yellow dots.
Behavior Reasonably peaceful. Can be kept with others in a community tank.
Feeding Mainly live foods. Takes dried foods.
Water conditions As described earlier.
Sexing Female less colorful than the male and also slightly smaller. The fins of the female are shorter and rounded and there is a black mark at the base of the dorsal.

Breeding As described above, genera *Aplocheilus* and *Oryzias*. Can be spawned either in pairs or in groups, e.g., two males with four or five females. Eggs hatch in 12-14 days at 78 °F.

Oryzias latipes (Schlegel 1850)
Popular name Geisha Girl Medaka, Japanese Medaka, or Ricefish.
Origin Japan.
Size 1½ inches.
Appearance A rather prosaic grayish-green fish kept mainly for its interesting breeding habit. Strains with a golden and reddish body color have also been developed.
Behavior A delicate fish unlikely to fare well in a community tank with more boisterous companions. Best kept with its own kind.
Feeding Accepts all foods.
Water conditions Moderately soft, slightly acid water to which approximately 1 level teaspoonful of salt per 3 gallons of water is added. Temperature range 75 °F.-80 °F. Does best at 78 °F.
Sexing Females are plumper and have shorter, rounder fins.
Breeding Set up as described above, genera *Aplocheilus* and *Oryzias*. Can be spawned in pairs or in small groups. Since parents molest neither eggs nor fry, breeding is a simple matter of feeding parents adequately and collecting fry as they hatch out for rearing in separate tanks. Breeding behavior particularly interesting.

After the male and female have come together the fertilized eggs are carried on the ventral surface of the female attached by a fine mucoid thread for many hours before they are brushed off on plants. Eggs hatch in 10-14 days.

Genus Aphyosemion (African Tooth-Carps)

This genus contains many brilliantly colored fishes which unfortunately fare rather poorly in community tanks. Under such circumstances they go about with folded fins, hide in corners, and rarely last very long. To appreciate the breath-taking beauty of these fishes it is best to give each species a separate tank. Further, in many of the larger species the males are so aggressive toward each other that it is best to keep only one male with three or four females. The tank should be placed in a shaded position and surface-floating plants provided. The bottom is best covered with well-washed scalded peat.

All species thrive in slightly acid soft to moderately hard water, although some of them have occasionally been bred in somewhat hard alkaline waters. Most authors recommend the addition of 1 teaspoonful of salt per gallon of water.

In nature these fishes often occur in small pools or drainage ditches, which in some instances dry up during the summer. Survival of the species in such instances is assured by eggs lying dormant in the damp mud at the bottom of the pond. Although adults die, when the rains come the young hatch out and carry on the species.

As far as their breeding habits in the aquarium are concerned it is customary to divide these fishes into two or three groups: (1) Surface spawners, which lay adhesive eggs on floating plants; (2) Midlevel spawners, which lay eggs on fine-leaved plants in the tank; (3) Bottom spawners, which lay eggs on the bottom of the tank in the peat or other medium provided.

Convenient though such a division is for descriptive purposes, it must be clearly recognized that this is an arbitrary division and that in different circumstances not only the same species (e.g., *A. australe*) but even the same pair will at one time spawn at the surface and at another time on the bottom of the tank. Therefore two divisions: (1) The surface spawners and (2) The bottom spawners, are adequate for our purpose and we shall now proceed to study them in detail.

Breeding the Surface Spawners

For most species rather small all-glass tanks or even large battery jars are adequate. Larger species are better bred in larger conventional aquaria. A layer of scalded peat at the bottom and some floating plants or suspended nylon mops complete the breeding setup. A

Aphyosemion occidentale   43   *Aphyosemion arnoldi*

conditioned pair or a group comprising one male and two or three plump females is now introduced. Often spawning commences in a few hours or within a few minutes and continues for many days. The procedure from here on is the same as that described above for the genus *Aplocheilus* in that the parents are moved on to another tank or the eggs removed from the parents.

Surface-spawning *Aphyosemion* eggs usually hatch out in about 12 to 18 days at 76 °F. However, when stored in damp peat at lower temperatures (65 °F.) the hatching is considerably delayed, so that these eggs can be sent by post to fellow aquarists in other countries. At no stage should the peat dry out completely or the eggs will perish.

To hatch the eggs the peat is shaken in a quantity of soft water (or rainwater) and placed in a hatching tank, and the temperature raised to 75 °F. Some recommend adding acriflavine, others a quantity of infusoria culture to insure or hasten the hatching process. The rationale behind the latter suggestion is that in nature the dried-up pools containing eggs are covered with fallen leaves; when the rains come, a culture of bacteria and infusoria develops which in some way helps the disintegration of the rather tough egg shells.

Breeding the Bottom Spawners

The breeding habits of this group resemble that of the South American *Cynolebias* and *Pterolebias*. These fishes spawn after lying side by side on the surface of the peat at the bottom of the tank. The eggs are buried by lashing movements of body and fins, which stir up the peat. They as a rule do not burrow or sink into the bottom as do their South American counterparts.

The breeding set up for these fishes is very simple indeed. All that is needed is a small tank with some scalded peat at the bottom. Plants, floating or otherwise, may be added to make the fishes comfortable but this is not absolutely essential. The fishes, either a pair or a group, are next introduced and allowed to spawn for a week or so and then they are removed. The water from the tank is now carefully siphoned out with a fine tube, leaving the peat and eggs undisturbed. The peat is now allowed to dry out a bit (but not completely) by laying the covered tank aside (temperature 70 °F.) approximately for 2 to 3 weeks. The lumpy peat may now be removed from the bottom of the tank and the lumps broken up by hand and the peat and eggs can be stored for many months at about 65 °F. in a jam jar or other container. An occasional drop to 60 °F. does no harm, so transporting these eggs presents little difficulty. At the end of a further month or two (or even longer) the eggs can be hatched out by shaking the peat in water as described immediately above, Breeding the Surface Spawners.

Not all species need long resting periods or drying out. The important

point to note is that at no stage must the peat become completely dry or the temperature fall too low.

Aphyosemion australe (Rachow 1921)
Popular name   Lyretail Panchax, or Cape Lopez.
Origin   Cape Lopez, Gabon delta.
Size   2¼ inches.
Appearance   This is undoubtedly one of the most beautiful of aquarium fishes. Body color reddish brown peppered with red spots. The caudal fin of the male is lyre-shaped and brilliantly decorated with many colors.
Behavior   Can be kept in community tank with smaller species, but does best in a special tank with its own kind. Temperature 75°F.
Feeding   A favorite item of diet is whiteworms. Accepts dried foods.
Water conditions   Slightly acid, moderately soft water with or without salt as recommended for the genus (see above, *Aphyosemion*).
Sexing   Easily told at a glance for only the male has the lyretail.
Breeding   Easily accomplished even with young fishes 2 to 3 months old. This is a predominantly surface spawner and should be bred as described above, Genera *Aplocheilus* and *Oryzias*. Eggs hatch in 12 to 15 days at 75°F.

Aphyosemion gardneri
   (Boulenger 1911)
Popular name   Steel Blue Aphyosemion.
Origin   W. Africa.
Size   2¼ inches.

Appearance   The gorgeously colored male has a pale green body with red underside. Head and sides covered with many red streaks and spots. The female is olive brown in color and has smaller fins.
Behavior   Reasonably peaceful in a community tank, but do not show off well. Males aggressive to each other.
Feeding   Small live foods. Accepts dried foods.
Water conditions   Moderately soft, slightly acid water with salt added as described above, under genus *Aphyosemion*.
Sex   The more colorful males are easily picked out.
Breeding   Spawns on either surface plants or on peat bottom. Long resting period with drying out not absolutely essential. Eggs hatch in two to four weeks.

Aphyosemion sjoestedti (Lonnberg)
Popular name   Blue Gularis.
Origin   Cameroons, Niger delta.
Size   4½ inches.
Appearance   Another outstandingly beautiful *Aphyosemion* of very variable coloration. Usually the male has a predominantly blue or bluish green body with red or red-brown dorsum. Brilliant red and blue dots and streaks cover the fish. The brownish green female is less colorful and has smaller rounded fins.
Behavior   A hardy, pugnacious species but can be kept in the usual community tank when young or in company with

larger fishes when older. Temperature 72°F.-75°F.

Feeding This is a large carnivorous fish best fed in cichlid fashion with earthworms, Guppies, and other meaty foods. It will, however, accept some dried food.

Water conditions As described for the genus.

Sexing Already indicated under Appearance.

Breeding As described for the genus. A bottom spawner. Eggs hatch after one or two months at 75°F.

Genus Aplocheilichthys (African Tooth-Carps)

These fishes come from the Nile and tropical Africa. Most but not all of them are rather prosaic silvery or brownish fishes whose main attraction is that they have an iridescent area surmounting a rather large eye. Their breeding behavior and water requirements are similar to the *Oryzias* in that the fertilized eggs hang on the female for a while before they are brushed off onto plants. The parents do not molest the eggs and rarely eat the young. The breeding set up for *Oryzias latipes* will be found adequate in most instances (see above, *Oryzias latipes*).

Aplocheilichthys macrophthalmus
  (Meinken 1932)
Popular name Lampeyed Panchax.
Origin Lagos.

Size 1¼ inches.

Appearance Translucent silvery body. Large eye surmounted by iridescent bluish-green spot. A faintly iridescent longitudinal band runs across the fish.

Behavior A small peaceful species best kept as a school in a tank with dark bottom, fine-leaved vegetation, and a dim top light. Given such a setting, the iridescent spot glows like a lamp and the effect can be impressive.

Feeding Accepts all foods.

Water conditions Peat-filtered water that is neutral or slightly acid and moderately soft. 76°F.-78°F.

Sexing Males have more pointed fins, females slightly plumper.

Breeding Can be bred in pairs or in groups. The breeding setup is similar to that needed for *Oryzias* (see above, *Oryzias latipes*). They spawn over a period of several days and only a few young are produced. Eggs take about 10 days to hatch at 76°F. Fry grow very slowly.

Genus Epiplatys

These West African Cyprinodontidae are rather sluggish fishes, which bask at the surface of the water. They can, however, dart with lightning rapidity to seize their prey. They inhabit stagnant waters and are hence not comfortable if the water surface is continually disturbed by strong aeration or filtration. They do not need water as soft as do some of the other

Cyprinodonts; near neutral water of moderate hardness to which 1 teaspoonful of salt is added per three gallons of water is quite adequate. They do, however, prefer a somewhat warmer environment, between 78°F. and 82°F.

Their large mouth and Pike-like appearance clearly indicate their predatory nature and their unsuitability for community life with fishes less than a third their size.

Most of these fishes are easily bred. They lay hard-shelled adhesive eggs in surface vegetation, so the methods described for breeding surface spawners should be employed (see above, Genera *Aplocheilus* and *Oryzias*). Either a conditioned pair or one male and three or four females are used for spawning.

Most of these fishes leave the eggs alone but anything that moves is considered as food so the fry are in danger soon after they become free-swimming. For the same reason there should not be too great a disparity of size between the fry, or else the larger ones will devour their smaller brethren.

Epiplatys chaperi (Sauvage 1882)
Popular name Firemouth Epiplatys.
Origin West Africa.
Size 2 inches.
Appearance An attractive old favorite. This is an olive-green fish with a bluish sheen in places. The body bears approximately six black transverse bars. The main attraction here is the ruby-red throat of the male.

Behavior This fish can be kept in a community tank for it is of medium size and well behaved. The males are not quarrelsome so more than one can be kept in the tank.
Feeding Accepts all foods.
Water conditions Not critical. No salt needed. Breeds over a wide range of pH and hardness.
Sexing Female has rounded fins. Red throat coloration occurs only in males.
Breeding Two males and three or four females should be brought together in a 10 to 15-gallon tank furnished as described immediately above, under Genus *Epiplatys*. Prolific breeders, as many as 100-200 eggs may be laid by a female in one week. Eggs hatch in 9-11 days at 80°F.

Epiplatys sexfasciatus (Gill 1862)
Popular name Six-barred Epiplatys.
Origin Tropical West Africa.
Size 4 inches.
Appearance A greenish-yellow banded fish of Pike-like appearance.
Behavior Can be kept in community with fishes of similar size.
Feeding Mainly live meaty foods. Reluctant to accept fresh or dried foods.
Water conditions Neutral water of moderate hardness.
Sexing Females paler with rounded fins.
Breeding Use one male to three females. Procedure as described for genus. A surface spawner that lays 100-200 eggs which hatch in 10-14 days at 80°F.

Genus Nothobranchius

This genus contains short-lived fishes commonly referred to as annual fishes, for their usual life span is under one year.

In their native habitat (East and Central Africa) the pools and ditches they inhabit dry up during the hot season and the adult fishes die; the species survives, for eggs are laid in the mud at the bottom of the pool. This does not dry out completely even though the surface becomes dry and fissured. When the rainy season comes and the pools fill up with water, the fishes hatch out in a few minutes. They grow and mature at an amazing pace and start breeding in preparation for the next drought.

In the aquarium also, even though the water does not dry up, the fishes still rarely live over a year (usually more like six to eight months). Hence they must be bred each year to replace the parents. Sometimes this is difficult, for the youngsters fail to attain a size suitable for breeding.

At the moment our knowledge of the biology and breeding of Nothobranchius is rather scanty, but rapid strides have been made in recent years by aquarists who have specialized in looking after these fishes. There is little doubt that some of the most outstandingly colorful fishes belong to this genus and every effort should be made to learn more about them.

Nothobranchius guentheri
(Pfeffer 1893)
Popular name Gunther's Nothobranchius.
Origin East Africa.
Size 2 inches.
Appearance Predominant body color of the male is green with shades of brown, yellow, and blue. Scales edged with red. Tail vermilion red. Females yellowish brown with almost colorless fins.
Behavior Pugnacious. Best kept with own kind in pairs or in groups of one male to two or three females.
Feeding Live and fresh foods only.
Water conditions In natural state known to survive considerable changes in water chemistry and temperature. Usually kept in moderately soft, slightly acid peat water, with scalded peat at bottom of tank.
Sexing As described above.
Breeding A bottom spawner which breeds as described immediately above, under Genus *Nothobranchius*. Allow pair or trio to bury eggs in peat for seven to ten days. Dry off peat and store for three to four months at 70°F.-75°F. Hatch by adding rainwater.

Pachypanchax playfairi
(Gunther 1866)
Popular name Playfair's Panchax.
Origin East Africa, Seychelles, Madagascar.
Size 3 inches.
Appearance This is a yellowish-orange fish speckled with tiny red dots. An

interesting, perhaps unique feature is that the scales (especially along the back) in this species (particularly in the males) do not lie down flat as in other species. They stand slightly on end as if the fish were suffering from dropsy.

Behavior An aggressive fish unsuited for the community tank.

Feeding Mainly live foods. Will take dried foods.

Water conditions Moderately soft, slightly acid water. Temperature 76°F.-80°F.

Sexing Male more colorful, with larger fins.

Breeding A surface spawner that can be easily bred as described above, Genera *Aplocheilus* and *Oryzias*.

Genus Cynolebias (Central and South American Cyprinodontidae)

Members of this genus are annual fishes, very similar in breeding behavior to members of the genus *Nothobranchius* and some of the bottom-spawning *Aphyosemions*. The breeding setup required is similar to that needed for other bottom-spawning Cyprinodontidae and has already been dealt with (see above, Genus *Aphyosemion*). It only remains to point out some of the relevant details.

It is generally believed that soft acid water suits most *Cynolebias*; on the other hand it would be equally true to say that some of them at any rate are not too critical about water conditions. They can also tolerate a fairly wide temperature range but appear to do best at around 75°F. Most of them are gluttonous and need plenty of live food. They spawn readily when a suitable pair is brought together, the individuals diving deep into the peat at the bottom of the tank. Often they disappear from sight during this process. It follows, therefore, that a fairly deep layer of peat, 1½" or more, should be provided.

For good results it is essential to dry out the peat partially—not entirely—over a period of two weeks and allow the temperature to fall to about 72°F. The slightly damp peat can now be stored in plastic bags or jam jars for another 3 weeks or more. Hatching of eggs is accomplished by shaking peat in water, when fry appear in 1 to 2 hours.

Cynolebias bellotti
(Steindachner 1881)
Popular name Argentine Pearlfish.
Origin La Plata region.
Size 2 inches.
Appearance Deeply compressed body showing a predominantly dark blue coloration in the male. Numerous pearly-white spots on body and fins. Female less colorful, of a green-yellow hue.
Behavior A small but rather aggressive fish. Best kept in pairs, because of hostility among rival males.
Feeding Large amounts of live and fresh foods. May accept dried foods occasionally.

Cynolebias bellotti (female)　　　49　　　*Cynolebias bellotti* (male)

Sexing As described above.
Water conditions, Breeding As for genus (see immediately above, Genus *Cynolebias*).

Cynolebias nigripinnis (Regan 1912)
Popular name Black finned Pearlfish.
Origin Parana River in Argentina.
Size 1¾ inch.
Appearance Male has a velvety black body and fins covered with numerous light green or blue spots. Female is ochre-colored with irregular markings.
Behavior A delicate, fairly peaceful species.
Feeding Live and fresh foods.
Water conditions Moderately soft, slightly acid water.
Sexing As above.
Breeding As for genus (see Genus *Cynolebias*). Difficult to breed and rear young.

Genus Fundulus (North and Middle American Cyprinodontidae)

This widely distributed genus contains many species. They have an elongated, almost cylindrical body and a flattened head. They are popularly referred to as Killifishes or Top Minnows. The temperature and water requirements of different species, living as they do in such widely distributed habitats, is bound to show many differences. Some live in brackish or even sea water, others in fresh waters of varying composition. A few are happy at 78 °F.-80 °F. but most others are comfortable at fairly low temperatures (70 °F.) and do not tolerate our usual tropical tank temperatures for long. Hardiness and breeding urge are often enhanced by a drop in temperature for a few weeks.

Many species of *Fundulus* live at the surface; a few spend their time at the bottom or even in the mud. The surface-living varieties are distinguished by a conspicuous golden spot on the top of the head. They spawn among floating plants. Most of them will eat their own eggs and fry. Since only a few eggs are laid daily over a period of time, breeding them can be a tedious affair. The procedures for breeding surface spawners on plants or nylon mops described above under Genera *Aplocheilus* and *Oryzias* are also suitable for this genus.

Fundulus chrysotus
Popular name Golden Ear.
Origin Eastern coast of U.S.A. from South Carolina to Florida.
Size 3 inches.
Appearance An olive-green fish with numerous green and red spots on flanks and fins.
Behavior Can be kept in community tank with fish its own size.
Feeding Accepts all foods.
Water conditions Slightly brackish to fresh water (1 teaspoonful of salt to 3 gallons of water). Not critical regarding pH and hardness. Temperature 73 °F.-78 °F.

Sexing Females are paler and less colorful.
Breeding Lays a few eggs each day in thick bushy plants, which must be removed to separate tank for hatching. Eggs hatch in 8 to 12 days. See also breeding surface spawners above, under Genus *Aphyosemion.*

Fundulus heteroclitus (Linnaeus 1766)
Popular name Local or Bait Killie.
Origin Atlantic Coast from Canada to Mexico.
Size To 4½ inches.
Appearance Very variable. The male is often greenish-brown with transverse iridescent blue bands on flank. The female is ochre and only very faintly banded. Different varieties have yellowish or reddish fins.
Behavior Rather peaceful for such a large fish.
Feeding Accepts all foods.
Water conditions Hard alkaline water with salt added at the rate of one or two teaspoonfuls per gallon. Temperature dependent on origin, usually between 65°F.-72°F.
Sexing As above.
Breeding See breeding surface spawners above, under Genera *Aplocheilus* and *Oryzias.* Spawns over one or two weeks. Eggs hatch in 12 to 14 days.

Genus Rivulus

These Cyprinodontidae come from Southern U.S.A., Middle and South America. They have long cylindrical bodies and rounded fins. The females of many species show what is popularly known as the "rivulus spot." This is a dark spot surrounded by a lighter area on the upper edge of the caudal fin, which is also referred to as an eye spot or ocellus. The males are more brilliantly colored than females although it must be noted that many species are of a rather prosaic appearance.

Regarding temperature, most species do well between the usual 75°F. and 78°F. but they are tolerant to drops in temperatures to 60°F.

These fishes like a sunny, well-planted tank. Most of them are not at all critical regarding water conditions. In their native habitat *Rivulus* are known to jump out of the water and rest on floating plants. In the aquarium too they sometimes jump and adhere to the cover glass and stay there for many minutes before dropping back into the water. They spawn in surface vegetation and hence can be bred by methods described above, under Genera *Aplocheilus* and *Oryzias* and under Genus *Aphyosemion.*

If well fed they rarely molest the eggs, so breeding them is a fairly simple matter.

Rivulus cylindraceus (Poey 1861)
Popular name Green, Brown, or Cuban Rivulus.
Origin Cuba, Florida
Size Male 1¾ inches; Female 2 inches.
Appearance A greenish-brown fish,

with yellow to orange belly. The body is sprinkled with green and red spots.
Behavior Fairly peaceful, suitable for community tank.
Feeding Accepts all foods.
Water conditions Not critical. Usually bred in neutral to slightly acid, moderately soft water.
Sexing Ocellus on caudal peduncle of female.
Breeding A surface spawner (see above, under Genus *Aphyosemion.*) Best to breed with one male and two or three females; 100-150 eggs laid by female in about 8 days. Eggs hatch in 10-15 days at 78°F.

Rivulus urophthalmus (Gunther 1866)
Popular name Golden or Green Rivulus.
Origin From Guianas to lower Amazon region.
Size 2¼ inches.
Appearance At least two distinct color varieties exist. In one we have a brownish fish with rows of red spots on the side, and the female shows the rivulus spot. The other is a xanthic mutant. This is a golden-yellow fish in which the red spots are much better discerned. The female lacks the eye spot. There is less melanin in this fish; hence it can also be regarded as a partial albino. The eyes are, however, black.
Behavior All varieties fairly hardy and can be kept in a community tank.
Feeding Mainly live food but will accept some dried food.
Water conditions Neutral to slightly

acid water of moderate hardness.
Sexing In the brown variety the ocellus of the female is distinctive. In the golden variety the female carries very few small or no red spots on the body.
Breeding Similar to *Rivulus cylindraceus.*

Genera Poecilia and Xiphophorus (Livebearing Tooth-Carps)

These genera contain some of our most popular aquarium fishes: the Guppies, Mollies, Platies, and Swordtails. The former two have now been placed under the genus *Poecilia* and the latter two belong to the genus *Xiphophorus* (Rosen and Bailey 1963). Many other livebearing genera are known but are seldom seen in aquaria today. Wild specimens of *Poecilia* and *Xiphophorus* are also rarely obtainable for they have been superseded by many attractive aquarium-bred varieties and hybrids.

These fishes are not critical of water conditions. However, they do not like peaty water. Most do well in slightly alkaline, moderately hard to hard water at a temperature between 72° and 80°F.

The males and females are easily distinguished by the difference in the anal fin. In the male this fin is modified to form a rod-shaped copulatory organ called the gonopodium. This change may occur either early or late in life. At birth and for some time afterward the anal fin of both sexes is similar.

Differences in the structure of the gonopodium in different species have assisted classification. This organ is very mobile and can be moved forward, backward, and sideways in most species. In two genera, however (*Jenynsia* and *Anableps*), the gonopodium can be moved to one side only, i.e., either right or left. Since the genital opening of the females is also not centrally placed we find that males with right-moving gonopodia can mate only with females with left-sided genital openings and vice versa.

Once a female has been mated with a male, she can store the sperms and deliver a number of successive broods without any further contact with a male.

The gravid female is easily recognized by the distended abdomen and a large, usually black, crescentic or triangular area in front of the anal fin. This is known as the gravid spot. This is due to the black pigment on the peritoneum (a thin membrane which lines the abdominal wall and various internal organs) showing through the distended (hence thinned and rendered translucent) abdominal wall of the pregnant female.

In the Black Molly, of course, the intense black color of the abdominal wall, even when thinned as a result of advanced pregnancy, prevents a view of the peritoneum and hence no gravid spot is seen. In the albinos such as the albino Swordtails, red-eyed Red Swordtails, etc., the "gravid spot" of course lacks the black pigment for no black pigment is developed anywhere in the fish. The crescentic area here presents a pinkish appearance; just as the pink in the eye of the albino, this is due to the color of the blood seen in the vessels in this region. On closer examination (preferably with a light situated behind the fish), spherical translucent structures (eggs or developing embryos) can be seen in this area. In the Wagtail Platy again this area shows practically no black pigment; it presents a translucent golden-yellow appearance and fine black dots may be seen in this area when it is examined by transmitted light. These are the eyes of the developing embryos. The gravid spot is not an absolutely certain indication that a fish has been fertilized and is carrying young, for even virgin females at times show it. Finally, one may say that it is no proof of sex either, for the male *Xiphophorus variatus* shows a very well-marked dark spot but this to my knowledge is the only exception.

The period of gestation, that is to say the time interval elapsing between the fertilization of the egg and the delivery of the young, is very variable, in sharp contrast to the more definite gestation period of the higher vertebrates. One of the main factors influencing the period of gestation in these fishes appears to be temperature. The time taken also varies, of course, with species and with other factors but as a broad generalization one could say that the gestation period is usually 4 to 6 weeks, at a temperature of 78 °F. to 80 °F., but is extended to as

long as 8 to 10 weeks or more at a temperature of about 70 °F. The number of young produced is also very variable. This depends on the species and the size and age of the female. Most livebearers bear broods throughout the year but the tempo is slower in the winter. Mollies frequently pause delivering during this period.

Livebearers with similarly shaped gonopodia can be hybridized. Thus Platies will cross easily with Swordtails, and Guppies have been crossed with Mollies.

Besides the late maturation of some males, there is another situation that the aquarist sometimes encounters. A true female, i.e., one which has delivered numerous healthy youngsters, gradually develops a gonopodium and other external characteristics of a male (e.g., sword development in Swordtails) but these fishes, though they look like males, cannot function as such and do not father any progeny. It has been claimed that on occasion a fertile male may be produced by sex reversal from a true female but this is doubtful. The reverse change from male to female is also unknown.

Breeding Methods

The fact that one fertilization can suffice for the production of numerous successive broods must be borne in mind by the breeder. A female that is to be kept for mating later must be isolated from all other males; if this is not done—and even if the desired male is later introduced—one cannot be certain of the male parentage of the future progeny. Thus when line breeding the first step is to pick out those fishes whose anal fin begins to show signs of elongating into a gonopodium and separate them from the rest without any delay. Then when the separated males and females are mature the best male is mated to two or three of the best females by bringing them together in a well-planted tank with surface vegetation. If fed well, nothing more need be done for under such circumstances the parents will eat few if any young when they are delivered. All that needs doing now is to catch the youngsters and rear them in another tank. For serious breeding, however, the female should be isolated in a well-planted tank or a breeding trap to provide maximum security for the fry. Of these two the planted-tank method is the better, for while Guppies and Platies do not suffer much from a short stay in a breeding trap, Swordtails resent this treatment. Mollies should never be treated in this manner; the female may die or deliver young prematurely.

As a general rule the gravid female should be moved to the breeding trap or planted tank a week before delivery. Netting her too late may injure her or lead to premature delivery with resultant loss of young.

Poecilia latipinna (Le Sueur 1821)
(until recently *Mollienesia latipinna*)
Popular name Green Sailfin Molly.
Origin Southern and Gulf States of
U.S.A., ranging into Mexico.
Size 5 inches, in the aquarium just
under 4 inches.
Appearance This is the Molly usually
available to aquarists, *P. velifera* being
much more difficult to come by. Both
Mollies have large sail-like dorsals, that
in *P. latipinna* being smaller and much
less handsome (see *P. velifera* below).
The dorsal in *P. latipinna* is very
variable. In only a few specimens is it
fully developed. The body of the fish is
olive brown with a pearly or bluish
sheen in places.
Behavior Good community fish.
Feeding, Water conditions, and Sexing
As for *P. velifera*.
Breeding (See details of breeding
livebearers above, under Genera *Poecilia*
and *Xiphophorus*.) Large females may
produce just over 100 young, each
measuring approximately ⅓ inch in
length. Fry must have plenty of
swimming room. Large dorsals develop
in large outdoor pools, not in tanks.
Tank-bred males usually remain rather
small. Dorsal fin development occurs in
the second year.

   A good way of breeding these Mollies
is to set up a very large tank with half a
dozen or so large females and two or
three males. If the parents are well fed,
few if any babies are eaten. In this
method all that needs doing is to
remove the babies as they appear.

   The Black Molly is a melanistic phase
of the *latipinna* which breeds true.
There has been some hybridizing with
P. sphenops. These crosses may be
distinguished by the location of the
dorsal; the leading edge in *sphenops*
begins after the anal fin, in *latipinna* the
dorsal begins before the anal fin.

Poecilia reticulata (Peters 1859)
(until recently *Lebistes reticulatus*)
Popular name Guppy, or Millions Fish.
Origin Venezuela. Barbados, Trinidad,
Brazil, Guiana.
Size Males 1½ inches, Females 2
inches.
Appearance This fish shows a number
of forms and color variations, even in
the wild state. As a result of selective
breeding and crossing established
strains, a host of new strains have been
developed. These are largely classified
according to the color and finnage of
the male. The size and shape of the
caudal fin is of prime importance in this
respect. The terms used are self-
explanatory, e.g., Cofertail, Pintail,
Speartail, Robson (round tail), Top
Sword, Bottom Sword, Double Sword,
Lyretail, Deltatail, Flagtail, Scarftail,
and Veiltail.

   The varieties are also classified by
color and color patterns. Thus we have
Red, Green, Gold, Chain, Chinese,
Lace, Bird's Eye, and many others. It
will be readily appreciated that
permutations and combinations of
colors, color patterns, and fin forms
can, theoretically at least, yield endless

Poecilia reticulata (female)   55   *Poecilia reticulata* (male)

varieties or strains of Guppies. An amazing degree of success has already been achieved, for not only have large colorful males with flowing fins been developed but the size of the female has also been increased and in recent years females with enlarged colored caudal fins have been produced.

Behavior The popularity of the Guppy stems not only from its beauty but also from its almost unique hardiness and its impeccable behavior in the community tank. This is a peaceful, lively fish impossible to fault on any point. As is only to be expected, some of the highly inbred strains are not very hardy. Such strains should be kept on their own.

Feeding Here again Guppies are most accommodating. They will accept all foods at all levels of the tank. To rear firstclass specimens, however, they should be fed at least twice a day, preferably more often. The diet should also contain a fair amount of live and fresh foods.

Water conditions This fish is uncritical of water conditions or overcrowding. However, to produce fine specimens, well-planted tanks with ample swimming room should be provided. Temperature 74°F.-78°F. Tolerates temperatures down to 60°F.

Sexing As described earlier for *Poecilia*.

Breeding Techniques described above, under Genera *Poecilia* and *Xiphophorus*, for livebearers are adequate. Female Guppies tolerate life in plastic breeding traps better than other live bearers.

Poecilia sphenops (Cuvier and Valenciennes 1846)
(until recently *Mollienesia sphenops*)
Popular name Molly, or Sphenops Molly.
Origin Mexico to Colombia.
Size 3½ inches.

Many color varieties of *P. sphenops* occur. The common brownish-olive *sphenops* with a pale orange caudal fin is rarely seen. Very popular is an all-black variety called Perma-black, which breeds true in that it produces all black young or only occasionally produces a few speckled young. Black speckled Mollies are attractive fishes but are not

Captions for color photos
Two species, several subspecies, and a great many color varieties exist of the discus; this is an attractive form of Symphysodon aequifasciata; *p. 57. A male paradise fish,* Macropodus opercularis, *in spawning color below the bubblenest; photo by H. J. Richter; p. 58. An extremely colorful fancy goldfish,* Carassius auratus; *photo by Edward C. Taylor; p. 59. Comet platies,* Xiphophorus maculatus, *are one of the plainer varieties of the species; photo by Dr. Herbert R. Axelrod; p. 60. The ram,* Microgeophagus ramirezi, *is one of the most popular American cichlids; photo by H. J. Richter; p. 61. Neon tetras,* Paracheirodon innesi, *are an old favorite; photo by H. J. Richter; p. 62. Convict cichlids,* Cichlasoma nigrofasciatum, *guarding fry; photo by H. J. Richter; p. 63. Rasbora* heteromorpha, *the common rasbora or harlequin, is the most often seen and perhaps most colorful rasbora; photo by R. Zukal; p. 64.*

prized as they are looked upon as poor blacks. Yet another recently produced variety is an all-black Molly in which the dorsal is enlarged and the caudal lyre-shaped. This is the Lyretail Molly.

Another attractive but hard-to-come-by variety of *sphenops* is the Liberty Molly, which comes from Yucatan. It has a silvery-blue body. The dorsal and caudal fins are red and orange, streaked with black.

Behavior A good community fish. An ardent algae eater, which helps to keep plants clean.

Feeding All foods. Must have vegetable foods such as algae, lettuce, and spinach.

Water conditions Moderately hard to hard alkaline water. It is doubtful whether it is advantageous to add salt to the water for this species. Temperature 80°F.

Sexing Presence of gonopodium easily identifies the male.

Breeding See Breeding above, under Genera *Poecilia* and *Xiphophorus*. *P. sphenops* is easier to breed and rear than Sailfin Mollies. It is not as demanding in its water conditions or space requirements. A large female produces between 30 and 70 young. The Lyretail variety is probably even hardier than the Perma-black.

Poecilia velifera (Regan 1914) (until recently *Mollienesia velifera*)
Popular name Sailfin Molly.
Origin Coastal districts of Yucatan.
Size 5 inches in the wild, under 4½ inches in aquaria.

Appearance Chief interest lies in its saillike dorsal fin, which is larger than that borne by any other Molly. It has a fin ray count of approximately 18 while *P. latipinna* with the next largest dorsal fin has a count of approximately 13. The body of the fish is olive green with a bluish sheen. The body and fins are decorated with dark reticulations and spots.

Behavior Can be kept in a community tank, but best kept with its own kind in a large, well-planted, sunny tank.

Feeding Besides usual foods must have vegetable matter such as algae, spinach, or lettuce.

Water conditions Alkaline, moderately hard water to which salt has been added at the rate of 1 teaspoonful per 3 gallons. Temperature 80°F.

Sexing Females too have a large dorsal fin but this is very modest compared to the male. Best guide is the gonopodium of the male.

Breeding See above, under Genera *Poecilia* and *Xiphophorus*.

Xiphophorus helleri (Heckel 1848)
Popular name Swordtail.
Origin Mexico, Guatemala.
Size 3½ inches (excluding sword).
Appearance The wild variety (Green Swordtail) is now rarely seen in aquaria; it has been replaced by many very attractive color variations and hybrids with *X. maculatus*. The best known are (1) The Red Swordtail, whose origin is a mystery, but it probably arose as a cross between a Green Swordtail (*X.*

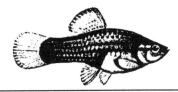

helleri) and a Red Platy (*X. maculatus*).
(2) Red-eyed Red Swordtail. Perhaps
the most attractive Swordtail. This is an
albinistic mutation. (Note: An albino is
an animal lacking the brownish-black
pigment melanin. It need not
necessarily be colorless.) (3) Albino
Swordtail. A pink or creamy fish with
pink eyes. (Again the black pigment is
gone but some yellow pigments
remains.) (4) Gold Swordtail. The body
color is yellow. Almost complete loss of
black pigment in the body. Eye black.
(5) Black Swordtail (red and green
varieties). Produced by crossing Red or
Green Swordtail with Black Platy (*X.
maculatus*). This strain is highly
susceptible to melanoma production. (6)
Berlin Swordtail. The posterior half of
this fish is black, the anterior red or
green. Produced by selective breeding
from progeny of black-sided or spotted
Platy with Red or Green Swordtail.
Very prone to melanoma production.
Wagtail Swordtail, red, yellow, or
green. From appropriate colored
Swordtail mated with similar colored
Wagtail Platy. (7) Simpson Hi-Fin
Swordtail. A mutant with an enlarged
dorsal fin.
Behavior Swordtails and their hybrids
are boisterous fish inclined to chase and
bully other fishes. They should be kept
with fairly large fishes only. All albino
mutants are distinctly less hardy and
less aggressive. (Terrestrial albino
animals, e.g., albino rats or mice, are
usually more jumpy and more likely to
bite than pigmented strains. This is

probably due to their poor eyesight.)
Feeding Accepts all food. Also browses
on algae.
Water conditions Slightly alkaline,
moderately hard water. Soft acid water
definitely inimical to growth and well-
being.
Sexing Presence of a gonopodium and
the "swordtail" permit easy
identification of males. For sex reversal
and other points of interest see above,
Genera *Poecilia* and *Xiphophorus*.
Breeding For methods see above,
Genera *Poecilia* and *Xiphophorus*. The
gravid female is best delivered in a
planted tank or a very large breeding
trap. Estimates as to number of babies
per brood vary. The maximum I have
personally noted is 180. Reports claim
that this can be as high as 250. The
usual number is more likely to be
between 50 and 100.

Xiphophorus maculatus
(Gunther 1866)
Popular name Platy.
Origin Mexico and Guatemala.
Size 2 inches.
Appearance This species is shorter and
chunkier than *X. helleri* and does not
bear a sword. Numerous varieties and
hybrids with *X. helleri* and *X. variatus*
have been developed. Some of the most
popular are Red, Gold, Blue, Black,
Tuxedo, Moon, Comet, Red-wag,
Yellow-wag, and Bleeding Heart. Like
the *X. variatus*, the *maculatus* Platies
have been bred in all color varieties
with elongated fins. These are called

"Topsails." Varieties with black fins are called "Wags."

Behavior Its size, attractive colors, peaceful disposition, and algae-nibbling habit make it an ideal community fish.

Feeding, Water conditions, Sexing, Breeding Same as for other livebearers. A good-sized female produces 25 to 80 young.

Xiphophorus variatus (Meek 1904)

Popular name Platy, or Variegated Platy.

Origin Southern Mexico.

Size 2 inches.

Appearance The males of the species have brilliant canary-yellow sides and red tails. The females are nondescript olive-green fish. The males commence to develop the colors rather late (4 to 6 months). Many strains have now been developed; the best known is called Sunset. As mentioned *variatus* with oversized fins have been developed and are called Topsails.

Behavior, Feeding, Water conditions, Sexing, Breeding Same as for *X. maculatus.*

Ambassidae (Glassfishes)

This family contains some very transparent-bodied fishes popularly called Glassfishes, most of which come from the sea or brackish water. Only one or two small fresh- or brackish-water Glassfishes are usually offered to the aquarist. One of the distinguishing characteristics of these species, which are sometimes mistaken by the novice for a Characin, is that the dorsal fin is in two parts separated by a deep notch.

Chanda ranga
(Hamilton-Buchanan 1822)

Popular name Indian Glassfish.

Origin India and Burma.

Size 2½ inches. Aquarium specimen 1¾ inches.

Appearance By transmitted light the body is transparent; by reflected light it shows many prismatic hues: yellow, gold, and blue.

Behavior Difficult to keep in a community tank.

Feeding Almost entirely small live foods.

Water conditions Hard (300 ppm) alkaline water (pH 8.2) to which is added 1 teaspoonful of salt per gallon. Temperature 80°F.

Sexing In the male the posterior edge of the posterior part of the dorsal and the caudal fin are edged with blue.

Breeding This fish spawns in plant thickets and lays adhesive eggs so it can be bred like Characins (see above, Characins) on fine-leaved plants or on nylon mops except of course that hard water as described above is used. These fish are not too difficult to spawn. About 200 eggs are laid and the parents usually leave them alone. They hatch in 12 hours and become free-swimming on the 3rd day. The fry are minute and very difficult to rear.

Nandidae

This family contains many predatory species with voracious appetites. They come from India, Burma, West Africa, and northern parts of South America. These stockily built fishes of robust appearance have large mouths. Some species can eat fishes half their own size.

The Nandids do best in dimly lit tanks with plenty of hiding places, which are best provided by suitably arranged rockwork to produce caves and arches.

Badis badis (Hamilton-Buchanan 1822)
Popular name Badis.
Origin India.
Size 2½ inches.
Appearance The coloration of this fish changes rapidly and frequently. The flank has a mosaic pattern, the usual colors being brown interspersed with patterns of red and black. From this the fish can change to patterns of greenish blue or pale pink.
Behavior Does well in community tanks with fishes its own size. This is not only the prettiest but also the best behaved Nandid with a not too large mouth. Aggressive toward its own kind, particularly at breeding time. This fish takes up queer attitudes in the aquarium.
Feeding Mainly live foods. May take some dried food.
Water conditions Neutral to alkaline, moderately hard to hard water.

Sexing Males hollow bellied, females slightly plumper.
Breeding Fairly easy. The fishes spawn Cichlid fashion (see below, Cichlidae) on the underside of a stone arch or flowerpot. The female is removed just after spawning, the male just after the fry become free-swimming. Usually a hundred or so fry are produced, which start squabbling and eating each other at an early age. Hence they must be graded for size, and plenty of shelter provided.

Monocirrhus polyacanthus
(Heckel 1840)
Popular name Leaffish.
Origin Amazon Basin
Size 3 inches.
Appearance The deep, strongly compressed body with serrated fins gives this fish the appearance of a leaf. This mimicry is further enhanced by its clay-colored sides surmounted by irregular black markings and a small fingerlike projection from the lower lip, which resembles a leaf stalk. This camouflage no doubt helps this slowly drifting predatory fish to capture its prey. The highly protrusile mouth opens out like a trumpet to an amazing size.
Behavior This is a species best kept with others of its own kind, in a well-planted tank.
Feeding This fish accepts little else besides live fishes about 1 to 1½ inches long. Since it can eat its own weight in food daily, the magnitude of the feeding

problem can be easily imagined. Water Tigers and Water Boatmen are also accepted.

Water conditions Soft, slightly acid water suits it best.

Sexing Not possible from external features.

Breeding This fish spawns Cichlid fashion (see below, Cichlidae) on flat stones, flowerpots, and broad-leaves plants. Eggs are fanned and looked after by the male. Young hatch in 3 to 4 days and are colorless at birth. Later they go through a stage when they are peppered with small spots resembling white spot disease, but this is a normal color pattern and disappears as the fish grow up.

Cichlidae

This family contains perchlike fishes that come almost entirely from Africa, Madagascar, South and Central America; only two species come from Southern India and Ceylon. The Cichlids differ from the Perches, among other things, in the fact that they have one instead of two nostrils on each side of the head.

For convenience of description it is best to divide these fishes into four arbitrary groups. (1) The large Cichlids, e.g., *Aequidens pulcher* and *Astronotus ocellatus;* (2) Dwarf Cichlids, e.g., *Microgeophagus ramirezi* and *Pelvicachromis pulcher;* (3) Mouth breeders, e.g., *Pseudocrenilabrus*

multicolor; and (4) The laterally flattened disclike Cichlids, e.g., *Pterophyllum* sp. and *Symphysodon* sp.

The large Cichlids are extremely interesting fishes but are unsuitable for the usual community aquarium. The dwarf Cichlids are reasonably peaceful and can be kept with other species of similar size. However, both have rather similar breeding habits so we will consider them together.

Large and Dwarf Cichlids

These highly evolved fishes show an elaborate premating behavior and care of the young. Any male will not as a rule mate readily with any female; an elaborate courtship is engaged in for the selection of a mate. It is, therefore, best to rear a group of them in a tank and let them select their own mates.

Most Cichlid males have longer and more pointed fins than the females. This is most marked in the dorsal fin. In older fishes this distinction tends to be blurred for some females too sport pointed rather than rounded fins.

Fish belonging to this group deposit their spawn on some hard, firm support. The actual type of support used varies with different species. Some like to spawn on the leaf of a broad-leaved plant such as giant Sagittaria or Amazon Sword, others prefer a flat piece of stone or glass wall of the aquarium, or they clear the gravel from an area on the bottom of the aquarium

and spawn on the slate or glass bottom; yet others like to spawn under tunnels or arches (a convenient way of providing these is by placing a flowerpot on its side or arranging rockwork to form an arch) or artifically prepared supports such as strips of plastic, slate, vitrolite (opaque colored glass) etc., set in some firm base. Sometimes they will even spawn on thermometers, thermostats, and other such objects in the aquarium. The type of object used as a rule varies not only with the species but also with the likes and dislikes of the particular pair in question.

Thus it will be observed that no hard and fast rules can be laid down; it is best to place in the tank two or three varieties of objects and let the fish choose the one they like. On the whole, dwarf Cichlids prefer to spawn under arches; the large Cichlids prefer flat stones.

Most of the Cichlids have been spawned in waters of widely different pH and hardness values. The spawning tank may therefore be filled with fresh tap water and the thermostat adjusted to 80 °F. Allow to stand for about 24 hours and then introduce the pair into the tank.

Spawning

At first both the parents clean the selected spawning site with their mouths, augmented in some instances by "sand blasting" achieved by shooting mouthfuls of gravel at the chosen site. Close observation of the pair will now show the formation of a translucent tubelike structure, usually longer and broader in the female and more pointed in the male, just in front of the anal fin. When the tubes are fully developed it is a sure sign that spawning is soon to commence. The female circles around the prepared spot and then traverses it, laying series of eggs close to one another but with a little space between them. The male follows and sprays the eggs with his sperm, thus fertilizing them. This process is repeated at intervals till hundreds of eggs are laid and fertilized.

When the spawning is completed there are three courses open to the aquarist. (1) He can let the fishes carry on looking after the eggs. (2) He can remove the object bearing the eggs. (3) He can remove the fishes. For the commercial breeder interested only in raising fish, one of the latter two methods is best; for the amateur the first one offers a chance to study the interesting behavior of his fish, which he would be ill advised to miss.

When spawning is completed the fish fan the eggs with their pectoral fins, causing fresh water to circulate over the eggs. This probably helps in the gaseous exchange, for eggs too respire, like fishes; it also prevents the accumulation of dirt and bacteria on the eggs. Maximum benefit is derived from these currents as eggs are laid separately, not touching one another,

thus exposing a larger surface to the water for gaseous exchange.

Fertile eggs usually have a clear, slightly amber tint but infertile eggs and those going bad for other reasons soon turn chalky white and if left for any length of time would become covered with fungus. The parents, however, rapidly remove such eggs.

It is particularly important at this stage to disturb the fish as little as possible. Even a trifling thing such as switching lights on and off, jarring the cover glass, observing the fish too long at too close quarters may upset them and result in the fish devouring the eggs. However, pairs vary considerably in the amount of interference they will tolerate.

After a variable time, usually about 3 to 4 days, the eggs hatch and the young are transferred to a pit dug in the gravel by the parents. They take turns at standing guard; while one is on duty the other either rests, searches for food, or digs fresh pits in the gravel. This vigil is maintained day and night. Every now and again the parents transfer the young to new pits. This they do by picking up the young in their mouths and, after performing some chewing movements, expelling them with some force into the new pit. It is believed that this action has a hygienic significance, for it cleanses the babies. The transfer to the new pit also helps, for any waste products are left behind in the old pit. The frequent change of the position of the nest may also have a strategic

significance in the wild state where the parents would have to defend the young from other fish.

At this stage the fry lying in the pit resemble a mass of vibrating jelly. This illusion is produced by the fry lying huddled together: some lying on their heads, others on their backs, vibrating their tails at a fairly rapid pace. This again creates a current of water, which probably serves the same purpose as the fanning currents produced by the parents earlier. At this stage the fish derive their nutrition from the large yolk sac which can easily be seen on closer inspection. Neither the mouth nor the gills have developed to a functional state. Gaseous exchange occurs through the skin.

As development advances the yolk sac is absorbed, the swim bladder begins to develop, and the fry become free-swimming. This as a rule occurs about the 8th to the 10th day. If at this stage the safety of the youngsters is of paramount importance, the adults should be removed; for though in the wild they would still have an important role to play in defending the young, in the aquarium their presence serves no useful purpose from this stage onward, and as a matter of fact constitutes a continual threat to the life of the young. However, as already mentioned, it is interesting to watch the breeding behavior of these fish and the aquarist is advised to take this risk, small with some species but very great with others.

When the fry become free-swimming

they swim among the parents in a tightly knit group, the integrity of which is maintained by a system of signals from parents to fry. This is one of the most intriquing behavior patterns to study; actions of the mouth and tail fin in certain ways produce water currents to which the fry respond by becoming virtually motionless, or coming together in a tight group. Any fry that wanders too far is picked up and shot back into the swarming school.

A few hours after the fry become free-swimming the aquarist should begin to provide food for them. Since they are fairly large they do not need infusoria; they can consume large quantities of newly hatched brine shrimps and microworms. A few days later, sifted *Daphnia* and Grindal worms may be given. If from now on sufficient amounts of live and fresh foods of gradually increasing size are available growth will be rapid. Meaty foods such as chopped earthworms and maggots, whiteworms, *Tubifex*, etc., should form a large part of the diet.

Hatching Cichlid Eggs Away from the Parents

Although this procedure deprives us of the opportunity to study our fishes, it is justifiable to do this if the fish repeatedly destroy their spawn or if we are interested only in rearing fry for commercial purposes.

The best procedure then is to remove the egg-laid stone or leaf to a small aquarium containing water similar to that in the spawning tank. It is advisable to set up gentle aeration around the eggs. The aerator stone should be so placed that the rising air bubbles draw a current of water over the surface of the eggs. It is neither necessary nor desirable to remove eggs that turn chalky white; any such attempt usually injures neighboring eggs. It is far better to add a few drops of methylene blue to the water so that these dead eggs do not get covered with fungus. The amount added is not critical. The water should be a fairly deep blue color. If too little is added, some fungus will develop and the dose can be stepped up. When the fry hatch out they collect in little groups resembling vibrating masses of jelly. These may be broken up now and again by sucking up and rejecting with a large-bore pipette with a rubber bulb.

Once the fry become free-swimming they are fed. The methylene blue will have almost disappeared by now; partial changes of water will remove the remainder. It is important to do this for brine shrimp will not live long with the dye in the water.

Finally, it remains to point out that none of the above mentioned adjuncts such as aeration or methylene blue is obligatory. Eggs have been hatched by just unceremoniously dumping them in a quantity of water (even a jam jar) without any further attention. This, however, does not detract from the

advice given earlier: chances of success are better in the majority of cases when methylene blue is added and aeration employed.

Microgeophagus ramirezi
(Myers and Harry 1948)
Popular names Ramirez' Dwarf Cichlid, or Ram
Origin Venezuela.
Size 2 inches.
Appearance Strongly compressed, thick-set body with a tall spiked (2nd spine) dorsal. Color difficult to describe. All tints of the rainbow can be discerned: rose, violet, blue, green, etc.; striking black band through head and eye and also in dorsal fin.
Behavior Very peaceful. Can be kept in ordinary community aquaria. Rather delicate. Rarely lives over 2½ years.
Feeding Accepts most of the usual foods.
Water conditions Best in moderately soft, slightly acid water. Temperature 78 °F.-80 °F. Some claim better results at 80 °F.-82 °F.
Sexing Difficult until they are mature, when it will be noticed that the male is more brilliantly colored, has a more pointed anal fin, and a longer black spike in the dorsal fin.
Breeding Typical Dwarf Cichlid. Lays eggs in pits, under arches, or occasionally even on flat stones. They hatch out in 3 days. Fry are free-swimming in about a week. Parents are unreliable, hence it is best to remove eggs and hatch elsewhere.

Astronotus ocellatus (Cuvier 1829)
Popular names Oscar, or Velvet Cichlid.
Origin Amazon, Guianas, Venezuela.
Size 12.5 inches.
Appearance Very variable, depending on strain, age, and condition. Skin matt, velvety, not reflectile like other Cichlids. Color, marbled olive brown to black with ivory, orange, and red splashes.
Behavior Surprisingly good-natured for a large Cichlid. Can be trained to take food from the hand and also stroked and petted.
Feeding Huge appetite. Likes food in large mouthfuls, e.g., live fish, chunks of beef, and earthworms.
Water conditions Not critical. Temperature 75 °F.-80 °F.
Sexing Difficult. Possible in large specimens when female fills with roe. Some males show three prominent round blotches at the base of the dorsal fin.
Breeding Specimens have to be over 6″ or so before they can be expected to breed; 500-1000 eggs laid on flat stone. Large tank (4-6 foot) needed with plenty of gravel and some flat stones but no plants. Good parents; as a rule they will not eat eggs or fry. First food, brine shrimps.

Pseudocrenilabrus multicolor
(Hilgendorf 1903)
Popular name Small or Egyptian Mouth-breeder.
Origin Eastern Africa, Lower Nile.
Size 3 inches.

Appearance Yellowish clay-colored body with gold and greenish iridescence in places. Blue spangles on fins.
Behavior Very peaceful for a Cichlid. Can be kept in community tank with fishes its own size. Becomes more aggressive at breeding time, particularly to its own kind.
Feeding Insect larvae, *Daphnia*, whiteworms; will take dried foods.
Water conditions Not critical. Temperature 78 °F.
Breeding Can be bred in small tanks (1 foot or over), when about 1½ inches long; 50 to 100 eggs are deposited in a shallow pit. After spawning, female takes up the eggs in her mouth. Male should now be removed. Mouth of female enlarged, stretched, and thin so that eggs can be seen in mouth. Fry hatch in 10 to 15 days, and emerge from mouth. Both female and fry should be fed now. Young return to the mouth of the female periodically, particularly at night and if danger threatens. First food for fry, brine shrimps. Female can be removed a day or two after fry start feeding.

Hemichromis bimaculatus
(Gill 1862)
Popular name Jewelfish, or Red Cichlid.
Origin Widely distributed, Central Africa.
Size 5 inches.
Appearance Compressed elongated body. During breeding season develops a remarkable fiery red color, particularly marked on the head. Numerous blue spangles all over body, particularly well developed on head and fins. Hence the name Jewelfish.
Behavior It would be difficult to find a more pugnacious or vicious aquarium fish. Adults must be kept singly or in pairs.
Feeding Earthworms, maggots, bits of meat.
Water conditions Not critical.
Sexing More pointed and elongated fins in male, who is also more jeweled, but the female may show a more intense red coloration.
Breeding As for all large Cichlids; about 300 eggs per spawning.

Pelvicachromis pulcher
(Boulenger 1911)
Popular name Dwarf Rainbow Cichlid, or Kribensis.
Origin West Africa, Congo.
Size Male 3¾ inches; female 2¾ inches.
Appearance Moderately compressed elongated body. General color green-gold to olive-brown. Ventral surface in belly region ivory and blue with large blood-red spot. Many color variations occur, even in fish from the same spawnings.
Behavior Usually peaceful, but aggressive at breeding time to own kind. Best kept in pairs.
Feeding Will eat all foods.
Water conditions Not critical. Neutral to slightly alkaline water of moderate hardness.

Sexing Easy. Female noticeably fatter. White abdomen with larger red spot extending almost to dorsum. Female more colorful than male. In young specimens sex can be distinguished by a crescentic golden-orange line in the upper part of the caudal fin of the male.

Breeding Easily bred typical Dwarf Cichlid. Prefers to spawn under arch; 100-300 eggs are laid, which hatch in 3 days. Young become free-swimming on 7th day and take brine shrimp as first food.

Pterophyllum (Species and Hybrids)

Three species or subspecies are recognized: *P. altum* Pellegrin 1903; *P. dumerilii* (Castlenau); *P. scalare* Lichtenstein 1822. The common aquarium Angel is *P. scalare*.

Popular name Angelfish, or Scalare.

Origin Amazon.

Size 5 inches.

Appearance Very deep, strongly compressed, almost discoid body with winglike dorsal and anal fins. Silver body with black bands, which become pale when the fish is frightened or kept in pale, unsuitable surroundings. In recent years many new varieties have appeared. However, only a few are commercially available. Of these the melanotic mutants have proved most popular. These include the Lace Angelfish showing a modest increase of pigmentation and the Black Angelfish showing extreme change in this direction. Mutants with elongated fins called Veiltail Angelfish, either ordinary Lace or Black, are frequently available.

Behavior One of the few Cichlids universally accepted as a community fish. However, only small specimens are really suitable for this purpose. Large specimens are aggressive to their own kind at breeding time.

Feeding All the usual food, including dried foods. Large specimens should have fair amount of live or meaty foods. Pregnant Guppies are commonly kept with Angelfish, for their fry provide a continuous supply of live food. Angelfish sometimes go on a hunger strike. This occurs when the fish has been maltreated or is frightened. It can also be a sign of internal disease. With care, choice foods, and frequent partial changes of tank water most fishes recover.

Water conditions Not critical.

Sexing Many minute differences have been described. Most of them are unreliable. A reasonably reliable method is to view the Angelfish from the front. Males are then seen to be thin and concave immediately above and behind the ventral fins, while females are fuller and convex in this region. Just before and during spawning the pointed slim genital tube identifies the male, the fat blunt cylindrical one the female.

Breeding It was once believed that acidic water was essential for success. Nevertheless today Angelfish are bred in both acid and alkaline, hard and soft waters. In order to breed Angelfish it is best to commence with half a dozen fish. When 10 to 15 months old, pairs will form. Each pair is then transferred to a 24 X 15 X 15 inch tank. Fish will spawn on broad-leaved plants or artificial spawn receptors made of vitriolite (opaque colored glass) or slate strips. Eggs can be left with parents or transferred to a small container for hatching as described above, Hatching Cichlid Eggs Away from the Parents. It has been found that although in some districts Angelfish will spawn freely, the eggs do not hatch, or if they do the fry die before they become free-swimming. The remedy is to transfer the eggs to distilled water (with a few drops of methylene blue added) for hatching, immediately after the spawning is completed. A delay of an hour or so can ruin almost every egg present.

When male and female Lace Angelfish are mated, ordinary Angelfish, Lace Angelfish, and Black Angelfish are produced. Mating two perfect blacks is difficult. When accomplished, it is reputed to produce all Black Angelfish. Both black mutations are weaker than ordinary Angelfish and have to be separated at an early age from normal Angelfish or they will not thrive. Good blacks are fully pigmented within a few weeks of birth.

Genus Symphysodon (Discus or Pompadour Fish)

This genus contains strongly compressed, disc-shaped Cichlids of a magnificence and beauty unparalleled by any other aquarium fish.

Unfortunately, so far they have proved difficult to keep and breed. Two species are recognized. These are listed below but it must be pointed out that much criticism has been levied against this classification.

Symphysodon aequifasciata aequifasciata Pellegrin 1904 Green Discus
S. aequifasciata axelrodi Schultz 1960 Brown Discus
S. aequifasciata haraldi Schultz 1960 Blue Discus
S. discus discus Heckel 1840 Red Discus
S. discus willischwartzi Burgess 1981 Willi Schwartz's Discus

Many records of successful breeding of Discus can be found in aquarium journals. As with other Cichlids, it is best to bring up a batch of youngsters and let them select their own mates. The spawning act is similar to that of *Pterophyllum* sp. Eggs are laid on a broad-leaved plant or flat stone. One or both parents fan and look after the eggs. The young hatch out and hang on mucoid threads. It is generally accepted that it is necessary to leave the brood with the parents, for once the yolk sac is absorbed the young feed off the mucous secretion from the bodies of the parents. Nevertheless, on one or two occasions fry resulting from eggs hatched away from the parents have been reared on fine, sifted, newly hatched brine shrimps.

Once this critical phase is over the young are quickly reared on usual foods.

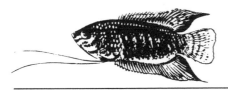
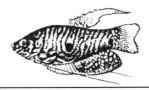

Symphysodon aequifasciata haraldi
Schultz 1960
Popular name Blue Discus.
Origin Amazon.
Size 6 inches.
Appearance Considered to be the most beautiful Discus. Body color brownish, traversed by dark blue vertical bars. The purplish head and body, particularly adjacent to the fins, is covered by numerous interrupted blue streaks.

Anabantoidei

The Anabantoids or Labyrinth Fishes come from Asia and Africa. Only the Asiatic ones have so far made popular aquarium fishes. This group contains old favorites such as the Fighting Fish and the Gouramies.

The special feature of this family is the labyrinth organ, which enables these fishes to use atmospheric oxygen. This organ, located in a diverticulum dorsal to the gill chamber, is composed of lamellae covered by a vascular epithelium. Atmospheric air taken in via the mouth is forced into the labyrinth, where it gives up O_2 and receives CO_2 from the blood stream. The spent air is discharged, usually via the gill chamber. This auxiliary breathing apparatus allows these fish to survive in polluted waters that would prove fatal to other fish and also to stand overcrowding and

life in small containers such as jam jars. If these fishes are prevented from coming to the surface they can still carry on respiration via the gills, but this is usually inadequate to maintain life. That these fish are very highly evolved is apparent not only from the presence of the labyrinth organ but also from their elaborate breeding habits. Eggs are not scattered haphazardly and devoured if opportunity to do so is available, but they are usually hatched and reared in a bubble nest built at the surface of the water. Some of the Anabantoids are mouth-breeders, e.g., *Betta picta*. The parental care of the Anabantoids, however, is a limited one and as a rule ends shortly after the young become free-swimming and leave the nest.

As a general rule, fights are likely to develop among the males at breeding time. This instinct is very highly developed in the Siamese Fighter, where it is virtually impossible to keep two males together in the same tank. Females also at times engage in mild skirmishes.

Nest Building

As already mentioned, these fish build a bubble nest at the surface of the water. Some, such as the Dwarf Gourami, incorporate filaments of algae or bits of plants among the bubbles to hold the nest together. The nest may be a compact structure composed of

thousands of bubbles piled high, or it may be no more than one or two layers of bubbles scattered haphazardly over the surface of the water. The nest is usually built by the male but in some species the females may assist in the process. The actual building of the nest is accomplished by the male standing just under the surface of the water and blowing bubbles. Each is covered with a film of saliva, which prevents the bubbles from bursting when they reach the surface. The mass of bubbles is sometimes piled up to 2 inches high over the surface of the water.

Spawning

The description that follows relates mainly to fighters; any differences between these and other Anabantoids will be noted as we go along.

In between spells of nest-building the male chases the female and engages in much fin-spreading and showing off of colors. At first the female retreats from these advances and seeks shelter among the rockwork or plants. But if she is ready to spawn she ultimately accompanies him to the nest. After a few such visits the actual spawning commences. The pair now take up a position just under the nest, the male curls himself around the female, and both begin to fall through the water, when a number of eggs are released by the female and fertilized by the male. The male now releases the female from

the embrace. Somewhat dazed, she reels around seeking her balance while the male rushes to the falling eggs, gathers them up in his mouth, and shoots them into the nest. This process is repeated numerous times until hundreds of eggs are placed in the nest. The spawning over, the male takes charge of the nest and its contents and usually drives the female away. She is liable to be hurt or even killed if she does not heed the warning and ventures too close to the nest. At this stage it is best to remove her and let the male look after the nest. Most Anabantoid males make good fathers and rarely eat the eggs. In some species, e.g., *Trichogaster leeri,* the eggs and fry float; in these the male can be removed if so desired. In others the eggs and fry drop to the bottom and the male continually returns them to the nest. In such species the male has to be employed to look after the nest, for any that fall to the bottom usually perish. Here the male must be kept in till the fry become free-swimming. However, if the male continually destroys eggs and young, these can be saved and reared by transferring to very shallow water (1 to 2 inches deep) and using mild aeration. Anabantoid fry are usually very small and difficult to rear.

Betta splendens (Regan 1909)
Popular name Siamese Fighting Fish.
Origin Malay, Thailand.
Size 2½ inches.
Appearance The wild species has been replaced by many aquarium-bred

strains, some with long fins and others with short fins. In the long-finned varieties, pure colors are highly prized. These are blue, green and red, although blends of these colors will also produce very beautiful fishes. A short-finned variety with a cream body and short rounded fins is referred to as the Cambodia Fighter. Other short-finned varieties are lavender opalines, where the body is a lavender color and the fins a deep sapphire blue. Similarly we have green opalines and multicolored opalines. Females are usually short-finned, rather drab creatures compared with the males.

Behavior The Fighting Fish derives its name from the fact that two males will fight each other as soon as they are brought together, tearing each other's fins but rarely if ever causing death. This is as far as their aggression goes. They do not fight other fishes and are frequently kept in community tanks. The only snag here is that the fish hangs about in a corner and rarely shows its full beauty. If one or two females are introduced, the male shows himself more often. Fully to appreciate this fish, one must have a number of male *Bettas* housed side by side in separate small glass tanks or jars. The display they then put on is something that no aquarist is likely to forget.

Feeding Accepts all foods but must have a fair amount of live and fresh foods.

Sexing Females more drab, short-finned, and plumper. The vent is everted, giving rise to an appearance suggesting that an egg is hanging out of the vent.

Breeding This is one of the easiest fishes to spawn. The only requirement is that both fishes should be really ready for breeding. The male indicates this by building a bubble nest. The female must be very plump. Aquarists describe this by saying "as if she has swallowed a marble." The breeding behavior and details have already been discussed (see immediately above, Anabantidae). The number of eggs laid in a spawning appears to be very variable: some accounts rate it as low as 100 to 200 eggs. I have obtained 250 to 400 fry per spawning on many occasions. The record number has been 960 fry reared from a single spawning. Important points to note are: (1) The male should not be removed until the fry become free-swimming (this takes about a week at 80 °F.), for most fry that fall to the bottom perish; (2) Copious supply of fine infusoria, for Fighter fry are one of the tiniest the aquarist encounters; (3) Keep glass cover on for fry are sensitive to cold drafts during the first 2 or 3 weeks of life; (4) Hold temperature steadily between 78 °F. and 80 °F. Large numbers will perish if temperature drops; (5) Separate fishes at an early stage for large numbers of good quality males can be reared only by intensive individual care and feeding. One-pound jam jars are adequate for this purpose; larger containers do not materially assist in this.

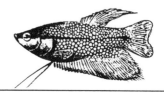

Colisa lalia (Hamilton-Buchanan 1822)
Popular name Dwarf Gourami.
Origin India.
Size 2 inches.
Appearance Strongly compressed oval body adorned with rows of blue and green spots on a red background.
Behavior A very peaceful species, but unfortunately of a rather shy and retiring nature, and very prone to dropsy and other ailments such as velvet disease.
Feeding Takes all foods, including dried foods.
Water conditions Not critical. Near neutral, moderately soft water.
Sexing The more brilliant coloring of the male makes sexing easy. The dorsal fin is elongated and pointed in the male, short and rounded in the female.
Breeding As described in family description; small compact nest containing bits of plants built by male; 200 to 300 eggs are laid, which hatch in 2 or 3 days. Fry become free-swimming on the 5th or 6th day. Fry are very small and difficult to rear. Even with abundant food and expert treatment, one cannot always raise large numbers from a spawning.

Trichogaster leeri (Bleeker 1852)
Popular name Pearl, or Mosaic Gourami.
Origin Malaya, Sumatra, Borneo.
Size 4½ inches.
Appearance Probably the most beautiful of all the Goramies. It has a long, strongly compressed, silvery iridescent body covered with numerous spots. Diffuse red coloration on ventral surface.
Behavior A very peaceful fish, ideal for community tanks.
Feeding All conventional foods, including dried foods.
Water conditions Not critical. Neutral to slightly alkaline, moderately hard water.
Sexing The dorsal and anal fins of the male are decidedly longer and more pointed than of the female. This can be detected in small specimens (2 inches). In large breeding-size fish (3 inches and over) the red "throat" of the male and the slightly fuller appearance of the female make sexing very easy. In the author's experience, adult males are usually difficult to come by.
Breeding This fish is late in maturing. Success is usually possible only with fairly large adult specimens. However, once a suitable pair is obtained, breeding large numbers of these fish is very easy. A large tank is set up in the usual way and a few floating plants should be provided. A large, rather diffuse bubble nest is built by this species; 500 eggs are laid which, being light, float to the surface. The fry hatch out in 2 days. Both male and female can be removed after spawning, since fry do not fall to the bottom. However, if you wish to observe the parental care, the male can be left in the tank until fry become free-swimming, on the 5th day. Fry need infusoria as first food. They grow at a very rapid rate if fed well.